Four Pillars of the Neo-Renaissance Man

*Self-Mastery
in the
Dark-Age of Decadence*

Eric S. Deslauriers

First Paperback Edition

Cover art and interior design by Eric S. Deslauriers

Cover image: *"Wanderer above the Sea of Fog"*
by Caspar David Friedrich (c. 1818)
Media file available on Wikimedia Commons

Copyright © 2019 Eric S. Deslauriers
All rights reserved.
ISBN: 9781093883831

Table of Contents

PROLOGUE: *THE DARK-AGE OF DECADENCE* **1**
    The Age of Comfort *1*
    The Siren Call of Distraction *2*
    The Dark-Age of Decadence *4*
    Mass Man *6*
    Inertial Man *7*
    The Neo-Peasant *8*
    The Noble Man *9*
    The Renaissance Man *11*
    The Neo-Renaissance Man *11*

INTRODUCTION **15**
    Self-Reflection *15*
    The Four Pillars *16*
    Eternal Principles *17*

THE FIRST PILLAR OF THE NEO-RENAISSANCE MAN: *RESPONSIBILITY* **21**
    The Mass Abdication of Responsibility *21*
    Categories of Responsibility *23*
    I. ECONOMIC RESPONSIBILITIES:
    SURVIVAL 25
        Entropy & Amnesia *25*
        Systemic Vulnerability *27*
    SELF-SUFFICIENCY 29
        The Dark-Age of Debt *29*
        The Mirage of Debt *30*
        Self-Sufficiency is Sovereignty *31*
    II. EXTRINSIC RESPONSIBILITIES 33
        "Open-Loops" *33*
        Avoidance *34*
        Task-Management *35*
    III. EXISTENTIAL RESPONSIBILITIES:
    INTERNAL LOCUS-OF-CONTROL 37

  The Cult of "Victimhood"...*38*
  Of "Two Minds"...*39*
  Stoic Equanimity..*40*
  Embracing Fate..*41*
 DEATH...*43*
  The Denial of Death..*43*
  The Paradox of Immortality..*44*
  Embracing Death...*46*
 CONCLUSION..*48*
  The Bedrock of Responsibility...*48*

THE SECOND PILLAR OF THE NEO-RENAISSANCE MAN: *VISION* **51**
  Categories of Vision..*52*
  Transcending the "Mundane"...*52*
 I. SELF-IMAGE..*54*
  Psycho-Cybernetics..*54*
  Identity Slavery..*55*
  Self-Esteem..*56*
  Becoming Who You Are...*58*
 II. IMAGINATION..*59*
  Lack of Imagination is Fatal..*59*
  Visualization..*60*
  Journaling..*61*
  Vision Precedes Mission..*62*
 III. LEGACY..*64*
  Who Will You "Be" After Death?.................................*64*
  The Cosmic Ledger..*65*
  The Monument of your Existence...................................*66*
  Legacy Inspires Desire...*67*
  The Perspective of Eternity..*67*
 CONCLUSION..*69*

THE THIRD PILLAR OF THE NEO-RENAISSANCE MAN: *MISSION* **71**
  Failure & Defeat..*71*
  On "Closure"..*72*
  Categories of Mission..*73*
 I. ARCH-MISSION...*74*
  Your Crusade...*74*
  Sacrifice & Austerity...*74*
  Mastery & Creation..*76*

  The Boy Within.. 77
  The Colossus of Your Life 77
  Mission & Purpose 78
  Karmic Gravity... 79
 II. TERTIARY MISSIONS 81
  Killing Time 81
  Harvesting Time... 82
  Constructive Relaxation 83
  Goals & Objectives 84
  Improvement 85
 III. RITUALS & RESOLUTIONS 86
  Habit is Destiny 86
 RITUALS... 88
  Eternal Missions 88
 RESOLUTIONS... 90
  Anti-Habits 90
  Addiction 91
 CONCLUSION 93
  From Boy to Warrior-King 93

THE FOURTH PILLAR OF THE NEO-RENAISSANCE MAN: *PURPOSE* 97
  The Omega-Point.. 97
  Destiny, Not Fate 98
  Categories of Purpose.. 100
 I. YOUR GIFT 101
  Mastery Is Never "Achieved" 101
  Mastery Is Not "Fun" 102
  The Nobility of Pain... 103
  Your Gift is Your Destiny... 104
 II. PERSONAL MYTHOLOGY 105
  "Why?".. 105
  The Myth of Sisyphus 106
  Nobility is Sisyphean 108
  Eternal Recurrence.. 109
  Regret 110
  Life Affirming Mythology 111
 III. META-PURPOSE... 113
  Elemental Purpose.. 113
  Evolution.. 114
  Retrogression and the Neo-Peasant................................ 114
  The Retrogression of the West.. 116

 Evolve!...*117*
 CONCLUSION 118
  Austerity...*118*
  Purpose is a Responsibility..*119*

AFTERWARD **121**
 The Ancient Tradition of Nobility..*121*
 Tough Love *123*
 Self-Mastery in the Age of Western Collapse *124*
 The Neo-Peasant..*125*
 The Neo-Renaissance Man..*126*
 The Eternal Principles of Self-Mastery....................................*127*

ACKNOWLEDGEMENTS **131**

ABOUT THE AUTHOR **133**

Dedicated to the *Last Men of the West*...

If there is any hope left for Western Civilization it resides within the few remaining Men of Nobility who proudly keep the flickering flame of its spirit alive in their hearts.

"If you refuse to let your own suffering lie upon you even for an hour, and if you constantly try to prevent and forestall all possible distress way ahead of time; if you experience suffering and displeasure as evil, hateful, worthy of annihilation, and as a defect of existence, then it is clear that you harbour in your heart the RELIGION OF COMFORTABLENESS. How little you know of human happiness, you comfortable people, for happiness and unhappiness are sisters and even twins that either grow up together, or as in your case, remain small together."

– *Friedrich Nietzsche*

Prologue:
The Dark-Age of Decadence

DECADENCE:
  i. the act or process of falling into an inferior condition or state; deterioration; decay;
  ii. moral degeneration or decay; turpitude;
  iii. unrestrained or excessive self-indulgence.

THE present epoch of Western Civilization is an age of historically unprecedented material abundance. Over the course of roughly two centuries, we have harnessed the power of millions of year's worth of condensed solar energy and bent it to our collective will: we created a civilization in which unparalleled comfort, convenience, and luxury is near universally accessible. By all appearances, it would seem that this is the *Golden Age of the West*.

The Age of Comfort

It is easy to take it for granted, just how luxurious life has become: climate controlling technology integrated into almost all buildings and transportation machinery; robotic slaves that exist for the singular purpose of dutifully washing your laundry and dishes; everything that you sit or rest on is soft, plush, and cushioned; if you feel pain, there is medication that will numb it; if you are numb, there is medication that will make you feel again; entertainment is available on-demand and in infinite quantity. All is provided for! No necessity is lacking. Every desire is seemingly fulfilled.

We are all of us children of this Great Age of Comfort. We live lavishly. The comforts and luxuries that we enjoy rival or exceed those enjoyed by legendary members of royalty in centuries past. Cleopatra may have enjoyed the luxury of having a dozen slaves billowing palm leaves at her, but in our era even a "poor" man enjoys the luxury of air-conditioning technology – and it works much better than slaves with palm leaves. The average man of this Age of Plenitude enjoys the lifestyle of a demigod compared to his ancestors who only a few centuries ago were probably impoverished peasants.

The Siren Call of Distraction

However, with such phenomenal lifestyle standards comes a subtle, insidious, danger: DISTRACTION. There is a television in every room, now. The average Westerner watches five or so hours of television a day. For the sake of emphasis: *the common man of our age spends almost a quarter of his day passively staring at a light and sound emitting amusement box.*

If we are not being hypnotized by the television, it is the computer screen that transfixes us. If not the computer screen, it is a small screen that fits in our pockets and is carried with us everywhere, at all times, and which stupefies us into a literal trance as we compulsively stare and tap at it every few minutes.

Prologue

It would be not an exaggeration to assert that many if not most Westerners today are on track to have *lived almost their entire lives vicariously through the medium of a screen*. "Virtual reality" is not a futuristic fantasy technology: we have already been almost totally subsumed within it, and we do not even seem to realize it. THE SCREEN is undoubtedly the monolithic symbol, the totem, of this Age of Distraction.

How alluring the siren call of *distraction* is, though! In Greek mythology, the Sirens were beautiful creatures, femme fatales, who distracted sailors with their hypnotic music and voices into shipwrecking themselves on the island of the Sirens. Indeed, how easy it is to laze in front of the television instead of "doing what must be done"; how comforting and maternal laziness can feel, like a spiritual cocoon shielding us from the harsh and burdensome responsibilities of life.

Videogames; junk-food; professional sportsball; the propagandistic mainstream media; a tsunami of pornography; alcohol and drugs; online shopping; social media and infinite scrolling: *distractions*, everywhere – all pervasive, bombarding us on every front, through every medium, by means of every sense. The Siren Call of Distraction: more cripplingly hypnotic than the Greeks ever imagined with their mythical seductresses. *Distraction* has spiritually shipwrecked more men of our era than Poseidon could ever lay claim to.

Never before in history has virtually the entire population of a civilization, cutting clear across every single socio-economic demographic, been able to live such lives of idle distraction and passive amusement. Once it was the case that only within a royal domain, like the Palace of Versailles, could such lifestyles of colossally frivolous diversion be observed: now there are suburbs and condominium complexes filled with millions of *Petit Palais de Distraction*.

The Dark-Age of Decadence

Despite the phenomenal wealth and technological dazzle of our epoch, we do not live in a "Golden Age". No, to the contrary: it would seem that a new Dark Age has furtively descended upon Western Civilization . . .

The Dark-Age of Decadence.

However, unlike the historical Dark-Age a millennium-and-a-half ago, in which toil and hardship represented the hallmark experience for the Western masses, *it is the softening caress of convenience, luxury, and comfort that has become the near universal condition of the average man in this Dark-Age of Decadence.*

In the last European Dark-Age, the West descended into comparative darkness following the collapse of the Roman Empire. There was no more "bread and circuses". For the masses during this Dark-Age, the promise of paradise after death was about the best one could hope for. If there were any distractions in those times, they were distractions from the grind of peasant life, and no one could blame a poor serf for indulging in what few pleasurable escapes he might be fortunate enough to savour.

In retrospect, the so-called European Dark-Age actually proved to be the percolating youth of a new European high-culture that eventually blossomed into what was to become the Renaissance Age.[1] However, from the perspective of the average peasant during the Dark-Age, there would have been little sense of *progression* or *momentum,* either civilizational or within the context of his own life. The stasis of poverty and toil was the general condition of the masses.

A "Dark Age" is fundamentally *inertial* in nature: it lacks the qualities of momentum, advancement and growth. In this Neo-Dark Age of ours, despite the astonishing material and technological wealth of our era, the average man remains as docile, passive, and inert as his distant Dark-Age peasant ancestors, but for different reasons: *the Dark-Age of Decadence is a diametric inversion of the last; this time it is self-indulgent luxury and comfort that stifles and oppresses, rather than poverty and toil.*

This is the critical distinction: the material and technological abundance of our age, that has enabled the contemporary masses to indulge in all the comforts, conveniences and luxuries of the aristocratic nobility of old, *has not at all enriched their lives or raised them into what could be considered a state of "nobility"*. Rather, this material and technological abundance has produced a generalized cultural decline, as well as spiritual poverty and moral bankruptcy: DECADENCE, in other words.

This is the epoch of the Dark-Age of Decadence because most men have been hypnotized into an inertial stupor due to the universalization of the ability to indulge in material hedonism. This is a "Dark Age" because the average man of our era is just as passive and docile as the

---

[1] Herein it is acknowledged that the term "Dark Age" is indeed no longer used in modern historiography to describe this period of European history, for many legitimate reasons; however, the connotations of 'civilizational decline' and 'cultural degradation' that the term "Dark Age" still popularly evokes remains relevant within the context of this book.

average peasant of over a millennium ago – except that it is *decadence* that has afflicted him in this particular cyclical iteration of history, rather than poverty.

The great paradox of the Dark-Age of Decadence is that, despite the blistering speed of technological advancement; the availability of vast quantities of energy-capital; and the protection of Western legal freedoms (for now), *most men have failed to leverage these advantages in order to pursue self-mastery or their own personal evolution*. Rather, the average man, exposed to the corrosive influence of material abundance that he is apparently incapable of managing responsibly, *has become a slave to it.*

For most men, there is little evidence of meaningful progression being made in their lives, despite the monumental leverage available to them in this late-stage civilization of ours. Most men are just so damned *comfortable* that their natural, masculine "will to power" has been all but extinguished. To avoid the spiritual misery of having to confront this pathological lack of ambition, legions of men have instead opted into the self-imposed serfdom of hedonism.

Mass Man

One early twentieth-century thinker anticipated the rise of this strange historical incarnation of a materially rich yet spiritual destitute "peasant" and named him, collectively, MASS MAN. In 1930, José Ortega y Gasset published his masterwork, *The Revolt of the Masses,* in which he described the ascent of this "Mass Man" in the West. Ortega's central premise was that "Society is always a dynamic unity of two component factors: minorities and masses…the mass is the average man." It was this 'average man', Ortega's infamous Mass Man, that he argued had come to dominate all social and political discourse in the West.

The problem with Mass Man, according to Ortega, is that the process of democratization following the liberal revolutions of the century previous, as well as the fall of several European monarchical dynasties in the aftermath of The Great War, *had placed the "common man" in a position of unprecedented power over the traditional minority of ambitious, high-achieving, excellence-striving men* – NOBLE MEN, as he called them.

Ortega argued that Mass Man's increasing domination of culture, society and politics was fatally stifling the ability of these "Noble Men" to maximally pursue their own self-mastery and personal evolution, to the colossal detriment of Western Civilization.

Inertial Man

Setting aside Ortega's political views, what exactly is it that characterizes his archetype of the Mass Man? Ortega writes:

> *"The common or inert life ... reclines statically upon itself, condemned to perpetual immobility, unless an external force compels it to come out of itself. Hence we apply the term mass to this kind of man – not so much because of his multitude as because of his inertia."*

Ortega describes Mass Man as being essentially INERTIAL in nature. Ortega did not arbitrarily choose this word: in physics, *inertia* is "a property of matter by which something that is not moving remains still and something that is moving goes at the same speed and in the same direction until another thing or force affects it."

The term Mass Man, as Ortega explains, therefore describes not merely the sheer numerical bulk of the population that Mass Man represents, but more crucially, *it describes the elementary lack of motion, energy, momentum, or velocity typified by his life.*

What is Mass Man's fatal flaw? He cannot initiate *action*. He may conceivably have some murky sense of a vision for his life, maybe a few hazy dreams or ill-defined goals, but due to the sheer inertia of years, even decades of sluggish inactivity, he cannot manage to initiate even the slightest measure of forward momentum toward the actualization of any of these flimsy ambitions. As Ortega describes:

> *"The majority of men are incapable of any other effort than that strictly imposed upon them as a reaction to external compulsion. And for that reason, the few individuals we have come across who are capable of a spontaneous and joyous effort stand out isolated, monumentalized, so to speak, in our experience."*

The Neo-Peasant

The Revolt of the Masses may by now be admittedly anachronistic in some regards, as Ortega was operating within the unique socio-political context of his historical era – as we all inevitably do. However, Ortega was certainly a visionary, and in many ways his book eerily anticipated what the prototype of his Mass Man would ultimately devolve into by the dawn of this third millennium . . .

THE NEO-PEASANT: *the contemporary incarnation of Ortega's Mass Man in the context of this Dark-Age of Decadence.*

All the material abundance, comfort, luxuries, and conveniences of this age have not elevated the average man to any measure of inner-nobility: it has all served only to pathologically *distract* him to the point of spiritual incapacitation. Indeed, Ortega's Mass Man has degenerated in our present historical era into this final, crystalline anti-form: *the Neo-Peasant.*

The Noble Man

> *"For there is no doubt that the most radical division that it is possible to make of humanity is that which splits it into two classes of creatures: those who make great demands on themselves, piling up difficulties and duties; and those who demand nothing special of themselves, but for whom to live is to be every moment what they already are, without imposing on themselves any effort towards perfection; mere buoys that float on the waves."*
>
> *– José Ortega y Gasset*

Ortega's Noble Man is the opposite of the Mass Man, or the Neo-Peasant in the context of this Dark-Age of Decadence. "Nobility," Ortega writes, "is synonymous with a life of effort, ever set on excelling oneself, in passing beyond what one is to what one sets up as a duty and an obligation."

The Noble Man is fundamentally the *Man of Action*. If the Neo-Peasant is an inert boulder that does not budge no matter how hard you push, the Noble Man is a boulder tumbling down a mountain at terminal velocity, impossible to stop without being crushed. The Noble Man does not require external compulsion in order to be motivated, disciplined and ambitious, for he internally generates his own vital spark of action.

The Noble Man recognizes that he is fundamentally responsible for creating, directing and maintaining the energy and momentum in his life. He knows that "no one is coming", as psychologist Nathaniel Brandon famously put it, and so he *definitively decides to assume full responsibility for manifesting his own destiny.* The Noble Man, at root, is the Man of Action . . . the Neo-Peasant, the Man of Inertia. Ortega:

> *"This is life lived as a discipline – the noble life. Nobility is defined by the demands it makes on us – by obligations, not rights. Noblesse oblige. 'To live as one likes is plebeian; the noble man aspires to order and law' (Goethe)."*

There are Noble Men in this Dark-Age of Decadence, though they are few in numbers. "These are the select men, the nobles," describes Ortega, "the only ones who are active and not merely reactive, for whom life is a perpetual striving, an incessant course of training. Training equals 'askesis'. These are the ascetics."

The *ascetics* of our age, the modern incarnations of Ortega's Noble Men, are not yet extinct, despite the corrupting influences of this Dark-Age of Decadence. While it is the Neo-Peasant that has come to dominate the cultural zeitgeist of our epoch, there yet remain a few Men of Action through which the Western tradition of ASCETIC-NOBILITY survives. These rare men belong to a spiritual lineage that can be most directly traced to the European Renaissance.

The Renaissance Man

Renaissance: a renewal of life, vigour, interest, etc.; rebirth; revival.

The dictionary definition of 'Renaissance Man' is "an outstandingly versatile, well-rounded person." This is what is colloquially communicated when someone is described as being a Renaissance Man. However, the deeper etymology of the term reveals that there is more to a Renaissance Man than simply being a "Jack-of-all-Trades."

The term Renaissance Man originates from the Italian expression UMO UIVERSALE. This concept of the "Universal Man" can be traced directly to a literal Renaissance Man, Leon Battista Alberti (d. 1472). Alberti described the Universal Man as one who "Can do all things . . . if he *wills*."

The original ideal of the Universal Man, or the Renaissance Man as we now commonly denote, refers to more than a man who has merely become proficient at several skills. There is something quite more substantial being communicated by the concept of the Umo Uiversale: The Renaissance Men, the original Umo Uiversale, *were those men who realized that the pursuit of self-mastery is a responsibility of nobility, not a consequence of it, and that personal evolution does not occur spontaneously in a vacuum, but rather requires discipline and iron will.*

The Neo-Renaissance Man

The *Umo Uiversale* of this Dark-Age of Decadence is THE NEO-RENAISSANCE MAN. If the Neo-Peasant is the contemporary embodiment of Ortega's Mass Man, The Neo-Renaissance Man is Ortega's Ascetic-Nobleman: *he who dedicates himself to the purpose of personal evolution and who commits himself to the lifelong path of pursuing self-mastery.*

The Neo-Renaissance Man rejects the anti-morality of the "Religion of Comfortableness" that Nietzsche ominously warned of. The worship of comfort, ease and idleness has depolarized and emasculated untold legions of Western men in our times. The Neo-Renaissance Man, in the context of his own life, strives to reverse this suicidal cultural trend toward decadence and decline, thereby escaping the inertial hell of the unambitious life lived only for hyper-stimulation and frivolous distraction. He is not the Neo-Peasant, in other words: *no, he is the man who has transcended the corrupting influences of his epoch and risen to become the iconoclastic director of his own life.*

The Neo-Renaissance Man is he who has committed to a permanent program of self-mastery and who strives ever toward the North Star of his personal evolution. The Neo-Renaissance Man embarks upon this literally endless journey because he believes that the ultimate purpose of life is to evolve: to become better today than you were yesterday, and better tomorrow than you are today.

Do not be a Neo-Peasant, mired in decadence, drowning in comfort, floundering in a quagmire of ease, convenience and luxury, to the point that one's life has sunk into a veritable swamp of negligence and regret. *Do not be defined by your historical era; do not allow the Dark-Age of Decadence to mould you in its twisted image.*

Aim toward higher ideals than the bulk consumption of shallow entertainment media; the false comfort of material luxuries; or the deceptive "safety" of the anti-ambitious life. Endeavour instead to be exceptional, rare, elite: indeed, dedicate your life toward nobility. *Become a Neo-Renaissance Man.*

Introduction

> *"You know from experience that in all your wanderings you have nowhere found the good life – not in logic, not in wealth, not in glory, not in indulgence: nowhere. Where then is it to be found? In doing what man's nature requires. And how is he to do this? By having principles to govern his impulses and actions."*
>
> – Marcus Aurelius

THE faults we perceive in others that we are most judgemental of are often the traits that we secretly fear most to discover in ourselves. If the prologue of this book seemed insensitive, insulting, or even elitist by way of labelling the average Western man of our era a "peasant", *it is only because those qualities that describe the archetype of the Neo-Peasant are traits that you may regrettably recognize in yourself.* If you are reading this book, it is probably because you strive to *become* a Neo-Renaissance Man, not because you already are one.

Self-Reflection

Perhaps you have or still continue to struggle with the innumerable temptations, distractions and diversions that proliferate in this Dark-Age of Decadence; possibly you suffer from a chronic sense of inertial "drag" in your life; maybe you, in fact, are or have lived a life characteristic of the Neo-Peasant that is so unsympathetically criticized herein – *but you have also a spark of life yet remaining within you that has not yet died:* you desire to break through the inertial influences of this Dark-Age of Decadence and into the accelerating momentum of a new paradigm for your life.

Four Pillars of the Neo-Renaissance Man is not the exclusive domain of already ambitious, successful men: rather, it is a guide for men whose souls quietly whisper to them in lonely moments of deafening spiritual silence: *"You are not following your Path . . ."* Most men ignore that inner voice. This book is for the men who do not.

This book is written for the man who may be all too familiar with the stagnant life of the Neo-Peasant in this Dark-Age of Decadence; it is for he who is hungry to *become* ambitious, who harbours a simmering ambition *to be* ambitious. This book was written for those men who may currently feel aimlessly adrift but whom nonetheless definitively endeavour to join the ranks of the few, the select, the noble: it is for he who wills to *become* a Neo-Renaissance Man.

The Four Pillars

The Four Pillars are a set of meta-principles that guide the life of the archetypal Neo-Renaissance Man. These are the core principles of self-mastery and personal evolution. These pillars are so fundamental to the architecture of a Neo-Renaissance Man's life that a compromise of the integrity of any one of them guarantees the collapse of the entire structure.

The Four Pillars of the Neo-Renaissance Man are:

I. RESPONSABILITY
II. VISION
III. MISSION
IV. PURPOSE

Each successive principle unlocks access to the next, and therefore the sequential order of the Four Pillars is not arbitrary. While all four principles can and should be respected and developed simultaneously, it is also the case that failure in one area is likely due to a failure to sufficiently master the principle preceding it.

The sequential nature of the Four Pillars may be visualized as an upward spiral, progressing from the grounded, concrete domains of biological survival or everyday responsibilities, and rising successively and ultimately to the metaphysical heights of existential purpose and "the meaning of life".

A man cannot possess creative Vision if he is not first a man of Responsibility; he cannot commit to a Mission if he does not have sufficient Vision to first create it; and a definitive sense of Purpose in life is impossible for he who fails to prove himself to be an effective Mission oriented man-of-action. Each principle inspires and breathes life into the next. Committing to a permanent program that aims for mastery of these Four Pillars is the essence what it means to *be* a Neo-Renaissance Man

Eternal Principles

The Four Pillars of the Neo-Renaissance Man are these eternal principles of self-mastery and personal evolution. They are not the product of market research or driven by consumer demand – in fact, quite the opposite, considering that what most men really want is just a "magic pill" to solve all their problems.

These four Prime Principles will not be sociological anachronisms a few years, decades or even centuries from the publication of this book. Even if all literature and records were to spontaneously vanish, even if we were forced to rediscover the intellectual and spiritual wisdom of the Western tradition again from scratch, the future Disciples of Self-Mastery (today, "Neo-Renaissance Men"; in the next epoch, a different incarnation) *would inevitably and invariably rediscover these Four Pillars and conclude that they are the fundamental principles that guide self-directed personal evolution.*

The idea of "The Neo-Renaissance Man" is merely a conceptual vehicle, a delivery mechanism for these Four Pillars, the fundamental principles of self-transformation. The purpose of this book is to reveal to men the transformative power of concentrating upon, committing to, and of *living* these master principles.

The ubiquitous material abundance of our present age has produced a spiritual famine in which the sacred pursuit of self-mastery and personal evolution are abandoned at the altar of the anti-values of comfort, pleasure and ease – Nietzsche's infamous "Religion of Comfortableness".

The Neo-Renaissance Man is he who escapes from this prison of historical determinism in order to fulfill *his* destiny rather than being subsumed into the pathology of the Dark-Age of Decadence. *The context of the era: unique. These principles of liberation: eternal.*

The First Pillar of the Neo-Renaissance Man:

Responsibility

THE Neo-Renaissance Man, first and foremost, is he who adopts a fundamental attitude of RESPONSIBILITY as the bedrock principle upon which the entire edifice of his life is built upon: this is the First Pillar of the Neo-Renaissance Man. It is impossible to become a disciple of self-mastery and personal evolution if one shirks the quintessential principle of Responsibility.

The Mass Abdication of Responsibility

The Dark-Age of Decadence coincides with the peak of a one hundred-fifty year era of exponentially expanding fossil fuel exploitation that has generated historically unprecedented material abundance. Western governments have leveraged this wealth to create vast "welfare" states, ensuring that virtually no one can die of anything but the most complete and utter failure of self-responsibility. *We live in an era in which men are no longer required to assume basic responsibility for their lives.*

Even a man who refuses to work for a living can nonetheless live a comfortable and luxurious lifestyle – at least compared to the quality of life of his not-so-distant peasant ancestors – if he merely exerts the minimum effort to exploit one of the countless capital-redistribution programs common in the West

In this Dark-Age of Decadence, men are no longer required *even by the biological necessities of survival* to respect the First Pillar of the Neo-Renaissance Man; the government will not let them starve despite their idleness, and will likely even subsidize their comfort and amusement.

A man who assumes zero responsibility in life will not only *not die* – as would have happened throughout most of history to anyone who decided to abdicate responsibility for their lives – but he will likely even be provided with a roof over his head, a welfare cheque to pay for pizza delivered to his door, and he will still have access to infinite quantities of on-demand entertainment with which to amuse himself.

Such cases of extreme economic parasitism are somewhat the exception – though certainly not rare – examples of the mass abdication of responsibility that is so characteristic of this Dark-Age of Decadence. More subtly, the Neo-Peasant's general propensity towards abandoning the principle of Responsibility is observed in his unthinking reliance upon external sources to provide him with the *spiritual* necessities of life: dreams and aspirations; goals and motivations; even his sense of purpose – the Neo-Peasant has outsourced the responsibility for generating all of these basic human spiritual needs to dubious parties with agendas of their own.

However, neither Madison Avenue nor Hollywood nor any federal agency can ever nourish a man's spirit by fiat: no amount of technology or energy-capital can be sufficiently manipulated into vitalizing and sustaining a man's *soul*. Thus, the Neo-Peasant's spiritual life is a desolate wasteland, even while his material world is cornucopian, due to his categorical failure to assume responsibility for nurturing his spiritual necessities.

The failure to respect the First Pillar of the Neo-Renaissance Man – that of Responsibility – is thus the chief cause of that miserable condition known as *psycho-spiritual inertia*. The Neo-Peasant lives a basically serf-like existence – static; immobile; unchanging; quietly miserable – *not* because this is his natural disposition, and not even solely because of the decadent life of perpetual stimulation, comfort, and ease that he lives: *rather, the root of his inertial malaise is fundamentally his avoidance of responsibility*.

Categories of Responsibility

The First Pillar of the Neo-Renaissance Man is divided into three broad categories:

- ECONOMIC: responsibilities imposed by nature and the finite availability of resources.

- EXTRINSIC: externally imposed responsibilities imposed by everyday life.

- EXISTENTIAL: psychological and spiritual responsibilities.

Each of these categories of Responsibility is qualitatively distinctive. On one end of the spectrum, "responsibility" is a grounded, objective reality of the physical world, and on the other, an abstract, metaphysical value. All three types of Responsibility are absolutely imperative to respect, however, if one's desire is to become that rarest of men, a self-master, and a man who has taken control of the process of his own evolution: *a Neo-Renaissance Man.*

i. Economic Responsibilities: *Survival*

The first Responsibility of every man – indeed, of every biological organism – is that of SURVIVAL. For our distant Neolithic ancestors, man's *only* responsibility was to survive. These men were responsible for themselves and to their tribe for providing food, shelter and security. If they failed, *everyone died*. Responsibility was not an abstract principle: it was life or death.

On this level, the First Pillar of the Neo-Renaissance Man is firmly objective. There is no such thing as self-delusion when it comes to biological survival. The biological system of your body is provided with the requisite fuel to continue functioning, or it is not; either you survive, or you starve to death. This is the immortal Law of Entropy.

Entropy & Amnesia

We are all *entropic energy systems*: we physically require a continuous input of externally derived energy in order to outpace entropic decay. Eventually, entropy wins this battle and we die – this is a law of the universe – but the Grim Reaper of Thermodynamics can be held off for years as long as we keep the energy input side of the equation positive. It is therefore quite plainly obvious that *the biological responsibility of every organism, even a single celled organism, is to absorb energy from its environment in order to continue living!*

While this fundamental fact remains as true today as it has since the dawn of carbon-based life itself, "civilization" has gradually eroded our awareness of this fact. Civilization is the phenomenon in which humans organize themselves into complex, mutually supporting networks that allow for specialization of economic production. As this economic division of labour complexifies, fewer and fewer men are required to participate in the actual hunting or harvesting of food. Instead, agricultural specialists produce the food, and then distribute it in exchange for goods and services of other specialists: cobblers; coders; professional warriors, and so on.

Eventually, civilizations may become so complex that this system that produces and allocates food, fuel, shelter, security, etc. becomes so far removed from everyday awareness that these finite resources are taken utterly for granted. It is just *assumed* that there is food at the grocery stores, and that there always will be. This is the psychological mindset of the masses in this Dark-Age of Decadence, presently.

Today, due to the energy super-charged nature of our epoch, Western man barely even needs to provide labour in exchange for basic necessities anymore. The basic necessities are so effectively provided for by the Western capitalist machine that finite resources have become akin to rain and sunshine in the minds of the masses. It all just *appears*, magically! Our system of central banking and fiat money is perhaps the most potent example of this delusion (more on this subject in the next chapter).

Indeed, these biological necessities are provided for so effectively by Western capitalism that their original, finite origin fades from conscious awareness altogether. The Second Law of Thermodynamics, which states that energy can neither be created nor destroyed, is forgotten. It then becomes unconsciously assumed – it becomes a paradigm, an unquestioned assumption about reality – *that our civilization is so technologically advanced that the physical laws of entropy do not apply to us.*

This sort of magical thinking permeates not only the minds of average citizens in this Dark-Age of Decadence, but has even come to infect political discourse and economic doctrine. Entire nation-states now operate on the delusional assumption that resources are limitless and that economic growth can accelerate infinitely and forever.

Systemic Vulnerability

The more complex a system is, however, the more devastating unpredictable systemic failures are to those who are dependent upon the system. Should this civilizational super-system ever experience a "glitch"; should the gears of the just-in-time logistics network ever jam; should the lights and the internet ever go dark . . . SURVIVAL would once again become the immediate responsibility of every man. The implications of entropic existence would no longer linger in the midnight of our subconscious: it would become all too real, once more, like entering the other side of the wall of a hurricane after passing through the calm eye of the storm.

The Neo-Renaissance Man is fundamentally a Man of Responsibility: he remembers, always, that food, fuel, shelter and security *are not* magical; they *do not* appear out of nowhere – *he is eternally aware of the entropic nature of reality.* The Neo-Renaissance Man is always aware that while *today* the basic necessities are blessedly abundant and accessible, *this might not always be the case.*

Four Pillars of the Neo-Renaissance Man

The Neo-Renaissance Man is conscious of the vulnerability of the system that produces and distributes the stunning wealth of this era, as well as the finite nature of the energy-capital that fuels it. He is also conscious of the fact that it could all grind to a halt at any time. He is aware that, one day, he might be required to once again, like the vast majority of his ancestors, *be directly responsible for his own survival.* The responsibility of survival is 'economics' in the extreme, where the balance sheet of life is divided not between credits and debits . . . but between life and death.

Economic Responsibilities: *Self-Sufficiency*

What our late-stage civilization does *not* necessarily provide every man with is personal financial SELF-SUFFICENCY. By definition, only a man *himself* may achieve the virtue of being considered economically self-sufficient. A responsible man must "live within his means," as the saying goes. In this context, what we are referring to is the notion of *taking responsibility for producing enough capital in order to justify the amount of resources you consume.* In other words, do not become trapped in the fatal spider's web of DEBT.

The Dark-Age of Debt

We undoubtedly live in the Dark-Age of Debt. Never before in world history has debt been as ubiquitous as it has become within the matrix of the present international financial system. Even what we commonly consider to be "money" is actually debt, with every central bank dollar that exists having being loaned into existence, and the interest owed silently compounds through the years and decades. Governments have taken advantage of this debt-based monetary system by rolling-over massive national debts from generation to generation, allowing the politicians of today to spend the capital of generations not yet born. *The influence of this debt-based economic paradigm upon the Dark-Age of Decadence cannot be understated.*

So much that is characteristic of this age of consumption is symptomatic of its inexorable intertwine with *debt*. Pathological consumerism is enabled by debt, even if it cannot be immediately afforded. That is the Faustian nature of debt, is it not? You can have anything you pre-qualify for, *now,* and you do not even have to work for it! This is the black magick of debt, and it represents a profound temptation on every scale: from the teenager who gets his first credit card to the superpower that buys stealth bombers by the dozen, debt is powerfully seductive.

Debt is a tool that *may* be employed strategically and productively, such as when it is used to bootstrap capital generating enterprises into operation. However, the type of debt we are referring to, the *unsustainable* sort, is the kind that is used to finance *non-productive consumption beyond one's ability to immediately afford*. What we are referring to is: credit-card debt; brand-new-car-every-three-years debt; monstrously bloated government budgets and bankrupt public welfare programs – any deficit expenditure that fuels frivolous consumption *or* which is economically unsustainable in nature.

The Mirage of Debt

The archetypical Neo-Peasant is inevitably attracted to this irresistible debt mirage because, from a distance, *debt shimmers with the attraction of a paradise in which you may gorge upon the seemingly infinite array of pleasures and luxuries so iconic of our age without having to earn them!* In reality, when the mirage dissolves and the sweltering heat of reality reasserts itself, the horror is revealed and it is the debt that gorges upon *you*.

I. Responsibility

The doomsday device of the Dark-Age of Decadence is *debt*. It enables and amplifies our ability to consume resources far beyond our actual capacity to afford. Debt is theoretically infinite, but real capital is not. *Resources are finite, and therefore so is our capacity to sustainably consume.*

The Neo-Peasant is not to blame for the creation of this sprawling, all-encompassing, all-consuming Empire of Debt, but his observable tendencies toward hedonistic material consumption is most certainly super-charged by the easy availability and accessibility of debt.

This debt-based financial paradigm is not sustainable, either on the macro scale of the central-banking/fiat monetary system, or on the micro scale of the irresponsible man who funds his self-destructive, drug-like addiction to consumption with credit cards, lines-of-credit, home equity loans, and so on. The Neo-Peasant is he who lives for today and today only, and therefore his meta-drug of choice is DEBT, which delivers as promised ... until it does not – and then the emotionless spectre of economic reality exacts its pound-of-flesh.

Self-Sufficiency is Sovereignty

The Neo-Renaissance Man takes seriously the notion that he is singularly responsible for ensuring that he is *financially self-sufficient*. Famous American author William Faulkner exercised his gifted writing ability and produced many classic novels in his lifetime, but he wrote them while working the nightshift at a local power station in order to support himself financially. You must become a financially self-sufficient man, even if the work that you must do has nothing to do with your grander Vision, Mission or Purpose – *even if it means that you must dig ditches by day in order to pursue your destiny by night.*

Becoming and remaining financially self-sufficient is ultimately a matter of self-respect. The Neo-Renaissance Man, after all, is no peasant, no serf, and no slave: he is independent; self-sovereign – a *free man*. How can a man consider himself to be traveling upon the path of self-mastery if he has locked himself into a dungeon of debt and thrown away the key? It is impossible.

The Neo-Renaissance Man, therefore, must respect this fundamental Responsibility: *he must be financially self-sufficient*. He absolutely is not required to be "rich", but he *must* ensure that he is not a debt slave. A Neo-Peasant is he who *chooses* slavery through debt. If this is you, if you have lived beyond your means, if you have been living an unsustainable lifestyle, if you have chosen economic slavery . . . then you have chosen the common path of the Neo-Peasant.

But you can change course, *now!* You can endeavour to accept this basic but essential responsibility: to live a financially sustainable, debt-free life. You can choose to become a Neo-Renaissance Man who *accumulates* capital instead of drowning in its counterfeit shadow.

No matter how dire your financial situation is presently, even if it will take years to become debt-free, the decisive *decision* to respect the First Pillar of the Neo-Renaissance Man occurs in the flash of an instant. You do not become a Neo-Renaissance Man when you finally are debt-free: *you become the Neo-Renaissance Man in that crystalline moment that you choose, definitively, the honest life of financial self-sufficiency.*

ii. Extrinsic Responsibilities

Ignoring even a small responsibility, like a simple obligation or chore, for a sufficiently long period of time is devastating to any sense of momentum that you may have had in your life. Avoid doing the dishes for long enough and your life will mysteriously slow to a crawl; you will lose all sense of ambition; everything except your favourite "escapes" will become a daunting struggle. Only a stimulating hit of entertainment or indulgence in other such distractions of our age will allow you to temporarily forget that your life has a sunk into a morass of neglect and disorder.

"Open-Loops"

"Open-loops" are pending obligations, duties, or tasks that you are responsible for that have not yet been completed.[2] Individual open-loops often seem innocuous because so many of the little chores and errands of everyday life are seemingly insignificant in the grand perspective. However, if too many of life's responsibilities are ignored they begin to silently converge into a psychic blackhole that siphons your energy, vitality and self-respect. Every open-loop that you choose to ignore is abandoned to the purgatory of your subconscious and will

---

[2] Productivity expert David Allen is the author of a book called *Getting Things Done*. Allen invented the open-loop concept herein explored and also synthesized the "Get Things Done" (GTD) organizational system that offers a systematic solution to the necessity of tracking all the open-loops that inevitably accumulate in life.

become a psychic parasite that feeds upon your continual inaction and avoidance.

Avoidance

This is exactly why Responsibility is the First Pillar of the Neo-Renaissance Man: you cannot create a Vision for your life; cannot fully engage your Missions; nor can you reliably connect with Purpose *if your energy is being drained by innumerable open-loops that you continue to avoid and ignore.* If you find yourself perpetually drained, lethargic, listless, passive, tired — suffering, in other words, from that unholy psycho-spiritual condition known as Inertia — ask yourself this specific question: *"What tasks am I currently ignoring?"*

Even the smallest open-loop can completely paralyze you. A simple household chore, if sufficiently ignored, can distract you for the entire day from doing anything productive at all. In fact, sustained avoidance of everyday duties and obligations can entirely derail the noblest ambitions and motivations, like a penny on the railroad track that derails a train billions of times heavier — and that is just the result of ignoring dirty dishes: imagine the psychically crippling effect that more critical open-loops are capable of inflicting if pathologically ignored and avoided.

If you are "stuck"; if you are suffering from a feeling of inertial "drag" — in other words, if you are living the life of a Neo-Peasant — *it is probably because you are avoiding certain responsibilities in your life,* maybe even deceptively small, seemingly insignificant ones. However, even if you repress these responsibilities into your subconscious, they will just condense into psychologically fatal singularities that cripple your will to pursue higher ideals such as self-mastery or your own personal evolution.

Task-Management

It is impossible to ever complete every task, chore or obligation that you are responsible for; there will always be new open-loops to replace the closed ones. The art of task management, therefore, *is not so much concerned with the completion of every task as it is the psychological acceptance of every responsibility.* Implementing and maintaining a task management system in order to assist with the administration of your life is therefore a transformative discipline.

Approach the administrative conduct of your life as a chief executive officer, a military general, or perhaps even a philosopher-king would. Men of great responsibility would never haphazardly start any day without knowing exactly what open-loops need to be closed; what objectives they must accomplish; who they must meet, and when; what the plan is for how their day fits into the rest of the week; what their goals for the month are – and so forth.

Men of Responsibility do not surrender the sacred potential of the day to external circumstances or the whims of their fickle emotions: they stoically acknowledge *what must be done* and do not lie to themselves about the true nature of their responsibilities. You cannot ever escape Responsibility – that is an adolescent delusion of the Neo-Peasant mindset. All that a man can do is accept the burden of his responsibilities with equanimity . . . and then *get to work*.

The Neo-Renaissance Man, no matter what domains he is responsible for professionally, administers his life as a man responsible for empires would. A task management system allows for open-loops to be consciously acknowledged and objectively tracked, which liberates psychic energy that may then be directed toward the grander strategic objectives in your life. The Neo-Renaissance Man's life is his Empire, and he, Emperor. Act like it. Adopt the daily discipline of relying upon a task management system to govern the logistics of your life and witness as ORDER transforms it.

I. Responsibility

iii. Existential Responsibilities:
Internal Locus-of-Control

"If your distress has some external cause, it is not the thing itself that troubles you, but your own judgement of it – and you can erase that immediately."

– Marcus Aurelius

"Taking responsibility", at root, refers to adopting what psychologists refer to as an INTERNAL LOCUS-OF-CONTROL. Most men, however, unwittingly adopt the psychological orientation of an *external locus-of-control*.

The Neo-Peasant of our age is he who lives at the mercy of external circumstance. Like a Dark-Age peasant chained to the fate of his feudal lord, *yet to whom the peasant is also entirely dependent upon for security,* the Neo-Peasant constantly blames the world for everything that goes wrong in his life, *while in the same instance being desperately dependent upon it to provide for his various needs.*

The Neo-Renaissance Man adopts the inverse attitude: he assumes personal responsibility for his reaction to external circumstances beyond his control, and for not being dependent upon external circumstances in the first place – to the degree that is practically possible. The Neo-Renaissance Man is an island of poised self-possession jutting from an ocean of blind circumstance. Most men drown in those churning, crashing waters, but the Neo-Renaissance Man is impervious: *he has adopted the psychological disposition of an internal locus-of-control.*

The Cult of "Victimhood"

Do not fall prey to the poisonous "victim mentality": the cult of victimhood is notorious for blaming external influences for everything that goes wrong in life while simultaneously being dependent upon external circumstances for the materialization of desires and dreams. This mentality is a form of slavish fatalism that prevents you from ever being able to become a disciple of self-mastery and personal evolution.

The cavalry is *not* on its way: if you are waiting for someone, something, or some fortuitous circumstance to "save" you, you are ceding control of your life to external forces that will either ignore or exploit you. No one is coming. No one will save you. If you entertain the fantasy that some nebulous happenstance will one day transform your life for the better, you are ceding control of your destiny to the whims of fate, *and fate is never generous to the passive.*

You must rewire your psychological orientation and adopt the permanent disposition of an internal locus-of-control. You must *take responsibility,* in other words, for generating and maintaining your desired life outcomes, as well as for reacting constructively towards obstacles and challenges that will inevitably arise and which are beyond your ability to control.

The external forces that exert their influence upon our lives can never, ever be fully controlled. Men build colossal dams, but the ancient and patient river knows that man's "control" of nature is but a temporary illusion that will always be violently dispelled in the final analysis. All that is truly within our control is our *attitude* towards circumstantial fate.

I. Responsibility

The first step toward escaping the cult of victimhood is to learn to identify with your internal locus-of-control: only then may a man begin to dissociate from being psychologically enslaved to the arbitrary flux of fate that we are subject to as mortal beings.

Of "Two Minds"

You have two minds: one of them is very effective at processing signals and stimuli received by your senses from the external environment. However, this very same mind also invents meaning about what it senses in order to construct a working model of reality.

Sometimes the stories that this mind constructs are just that: stories, tales – *fiction*. There is nothing true or real about these stories any more than it is true to claim "the colour green is bad". The phenomenon 'green' is neither good nor bad: it simply *is* – and if it seems to be otherwise so, that is because your mind has erroneously attached a false value to the object that it senses.

When we have a reflexive negative reaction towards a particular external circumstance, sometimes we cannot help it: our computer-mind has created an interpretation of the event in order to rapidly make sense of it. This is what the brain is programmed to do, and with good reason: it would have been fatal for our distant ancestors to sceptically question whether the ominous sound of cracking branches and rustling leaves in the inky darkness of night was *really* a predator or not. Such hesitation would have been a death sentence.

However, negative interpretations of the external circumstances that affect us are sometimes more harmful than the actual event. It is painful to lift weights, for example, but that pain is *good* because it means you will become stronger. Stopping as soon as you feel pain would be "logical", in a certain sense, but there is another part of you that decides that strength is a more important value than avoiding pain.

This is why identifying with our 'higher-mind', our spirit-mind, opposed to our 'lower-mind', the computer-mind, becomes critical. The spirit-mind is the mind that objectively *observes* the brain's automatic interpretation of signals from the environment and *decides* what attitude to adopt – factoring personal values, goals and ambitions into the equation – rather than blindly accepting the brain's initial interpretation of events.

Stoic Equanimity

There is an old Zen parable concerning a poor farmer whose only horse runs away. "Oh how horrible your luck is," his neighbours console. But the farmer responds: "We shall see . . ." A month later, the horse comes galloping back to the farmer, and with two healthy horses following it. "You have three horses now, when you thought you had none," the farmer's neighbours celebrate. "How wonderful!" But the farmer shrugs and replies: "We shall see . . . " A little while later, the farmer's son is training one of the new horses when he is thrown off the horse and breaks a leg. "How awful," decry the neighbours. "We shall see," replies the farmer . . . The next day, soldiers come through the village looking for military-aged males to conscript, and the son is exempted because his leg is broken. "How fortuitous," the neighbours proclaim . . . "We shall see."

The ability to maintain stoic composure in the face of adversity is a cardinal responsibility of any self-sovereign man. The ability to decide how you will react to and interpret external circumstances, rather than merely relying upon initial emotional reactions, is the responsibility of every Neo-Renaissance Man. To commit to the path of self-mastery, to desire to become the rare man of this Dark-Age of Decadence who rises above his chaotic animal passions in order to seize the throne of sovereign self-command, *you simply must accept the great responsibility of developing the mature, classically masculine disposition of maintaining a fundamentally inner locus-of-control.*

If ever you feel that you are beginning to "lose control", that external stimuli and circumstances are beginning to overwhelm you, stop everything – even if what you are doing at the time is productive – and find a mirror. Stand in front of it. Now stare into your eyes. Do not move, do not fidget, and do not flinch. *Now stare into the eyes of your creator*: this man standing at attention in front of you, *he is in control* – not of everything that happens to him, *but of how he reacts to everything that happens to him.* Gaze into your eyes and internalize this mentality until you have regained your noble sense of stoic equanimity.

Embracing Fate

FATE is the uncontrollable forces of the universe. Fate is often the harbinger of tragedy and disaster. Yet, the Neo-Renaissance Man embraces fate – in fact, he loves fate, *because hardship, pain, suffering, and failure are the spiritual materiel of greatness, the building blocks of nobility.*

The Neo-Renaissance Man is indomitably in control of his *reaction* toward fate, and that is why he does not yield to the eternal assault conducted against him by the forces of adversity, hardship and tragedy. Such an attitude of radical self-possession is a responsibility, though: you must *choose* to assume a resolute inner locus-of-control...

or otherwise doom yourself to forever be psychologically adrift in the stormy seas of fate.

Existential Responsibilities:
Death

Death is a great responsibility because life – human life, no less – is so precious, fragile and rare. Death is a privilege for it means you had the opportunity to live. The prospect of our imminent deaths should therefore serve to crystallize our commitment to becoming Neo-Renaissance Men. You want to die on The Path – not in the ditch!

The fact that you will die bestows an incredible responsibility upon you to commit to becoming a Neo-Renaissance Man . . . *now*. In *The Tibetan Book of the Dead*, an ancient Buddhist text, it is written: "Now, having obtained a precious human body, this one time, I do not have the luxury of remaining on a distracted path." No, you do not. Instead, you have the Responsibility of committing to being a Neo-Renaissance Man: to living a life that stands in rebellious defiance of inevitable death.

The Denial of Death

In contrast to the Neo-Renaissance Man's courageous awareness and acceptance of death, the Neo-Peasant is he who secretly *denies* its reality, at least as it applies to himself. The evidence for this denial is observed in the behaviour of most men: not in their words, but in their actions – *for the conduct of most men betrays that they actually harbour the secret, subconscious belief that they are immortal.*

This death denying man is not consciously aware of this denial, though: he still pays for life insurance; he still wears a seatbelt – but on a deep, subconscious level, he has failed to internalize the reality of his own mortality. This subconscious belief distorts and corrupts life in subtle yet profound ways.

The Paradox of Immortality

Imagine life as an immortal being. An immortal never has to actually do anything "now": if an immortal wishes to someday climb a mountain, he does not have to do it today because he has all the time in the world – literally – to do it later. Therefore, an immortal man could *justifiably* laze on the couch watching television all day instead of taking action to climb that mountain: the mountain is not going anywhere, and neither is he – *he is immortal.*

The paradox of an immortal existence is that an immortal would never be compelled towards action in the present moment, ever, *because there would always be an infinite amount of time to take action later,* even after an infinite amount of time has already passed. An immortal being is therefore expected to be *characteristically passive, unmotivated and lazy* . . . does this description sound familiar?

The Neo-Peasant lives with exactly the same attitude as an immortal: both are habitually passive, always delaying action for "later", until a "tomorrow" that never comes, always deferring action to that abyss known as "someday". *The Neo-Peasant acts as if he is never going to die: he acts as if he is immortal.*

The Neo-Peasant harbours this attitude in every context of his life. He is a pathological procrastinator in every environment he finds himself placed in. He has no ambition, and of course not: *an immortal does not require ambition*; an immortal can commit to manifesting his ambitions into reality by taking action *later*, for there always will be another "tomorrow" when you are immortal.

Again, it must be emphasized that the Neo-Peasant does not consciously deny his mortality. He knows, logically, as a dispassionate fact that has no bearing or influence on his life, that he will one day die. On a deep, subconscious level however, the Neo-Peasant is so inundated with distractions of all varieties, so drowning in the pleasures and comforts that are synonymous with this Dark-Age of Decadence, that he does not actually *believe* that he is going to die, on an internalized level.

Of course the Neo-Peasant lacks ambition, motivation, drive, imagination, courage, and above all the attitude of desiring to evolve as a man. *Of course* he does not exude any of these values or exemplify any of these behaviours! If you are immortal, if you are not going to ever die, there is no urgency – you can always conquer "later". If you are immortal, there is no need to bother becoming a Neo-Renaissance Man today as you can get around to pursuing self-mastery and personal evolution in some later cosmic cycle of eternity.

The everyday behaviour of most men is the barometer for their level of conscious awareness of their own mortality. Evidently, it would seem, most men subconsciously deny death. *He who proves, through his actions and conduct, that he is vividly aware of his own imminent death is a rare specimen of a man.* The proof either way is observed in behaviour. The Neo-Peasant acts as if he is going to live forever, while the Neo-Renaissance Man acts as if he will die – *because he will.*

Embracing Death

There is one more qualitative difference between these divergent attitudes towards death, and it is perhaps the most radical of all: the Neo-Renaissance Man not only accepts the fact of his own morality, *he welcomes it*. He is joyous that he is blessed with the gift of mortality, for he is keenly aware of just how static and inert the existence of an immortal being would be. It is not Man who is cursed with mortality: *it is the Gods who are cursed with immortality.*

Alan Watts, a scholar who very effectively translated Eastern Zen concepts for lay Westerners, once proposed the following thought experiment:

Imagine you are an immortal, omnipotent god. You can do everything, you know everything, and you have all the time to do and learn everything and anything an infinite number of times, over and over again. Eventually, inevitably, this existence becomes dissatisfying, *as there is no challenge, and therefore no possibility of triumph.*

So eventually, Watts postulates, being the god that you are, you conjure into existence a box with a button inscribed with a question mark. You, the god, press the button . . . *and here you are*. Let that thought marinate in your mind for a moment. Just like that, *here you are*, a mortal human, reading these very words in this exact moment, a being engaged in the greatest game imaginable: living the life of a mortal, destined to die, yes, but a being now capable of true and authentic *triumph*.

Death is a gift, for it means that we are not condemned to the static, stagnant hell of the immortals. However, it is a gift that comes with tremendous responsibility: if we are to die, potentially at any moment, *we cannot delay living life any longer.*

I. Responsibility

If we are mortal, there is an existential urgency attached to every day, every hour, every waking moment of existence. If greatness in life is to approached; if the discipline of self-mastery is to be adopted as a permanent, sacred practice; and if the evolution of one's self is to be pursued relentlessly, *the reality of our mortality urgently presses us to attack now, to strike now, to begin living the life of the rare Neo-Renaissance Men that we strive to be, now!* The responsibility of being subject to death is to live life with such fullness, passion and ferocity that only the spectre of death itself could possibly have motivated.

Conclusion

The Neo-Peasant is characteristically *irresponsible*. Why? Does the ubiquitous comfort, ease, and security that surround him – like the water surrounding a fish – *cause* the Neo-Peasant to ignore the various responsibilities of his life? Or do the various responsibilities of his life cumulate into such an overwhelming crescendo of pressure and obligations that he is driven to the anesthetising effects of self-annihilating decadence? Perhaps the question is merely academic.

The Bedrock of Responsibility

What matters is living a life of *radical responsibility*: this is the First Pillar of the Neo-Renaissance Man. Responsibility is the foundation that supports the structural integrity of the other three Pillars of the Neo-Renaissance Man: Vision, Mission and Purpose. Without Responsibility, these meta-principles are mere castles in the sand, fated to be washed away by the tides because they were not rooted in a firm base. *Responsibility is your bedrock*. You simply cannot ignore your responsibilities, as unglamorous and mundane as they so often may be. Wars may be fought for lofty ideals and abstract principles, but actual combat is always a bloody struggle in the mud.

At the end of each day, ask yourself: have you fulfilled your duties, responsibilities, commitments and obligations? If you are able to nod your head in silent affirmation, then you have lived a good day. If the answer is "no", if you dodged your commitments, avoided your responsibilities, then ask yourself: *what if you were to die this very day?* Behold all that you have left undone . . . No, always be "ready to die" by living a life of radical self-responsibility.

Responsibility: the First Pillar of the Neo-Renaissance Man. Even if a man does not imagine a Vision for his life; even if he does not establish a definitive Mission to execute; and even if a man neglects to pursue his deepest Purpose – *if only he succeeds at being definitively responsible, in every context of his life, he will still be among the rarest of men.*

The Second Pillar of the Neo-Renaissance Man:

Vision

THE second of the Four Pillars of the Neo-Renaissance Man is VISION. Once the First Pillar, that of Responsibility, has been fully internalized, access to the Second Pillar is psychologically unlocked. When a man is liberated from the inertial drag produced by pathologically avoiding his responsibilities, his creative faculty of Vision becomes uninhibited.

Most men in this Dark-Age of Decadence possess only the crudest sense of vision in their lives – so dim, so vague, that only in rare moments of clarity do they even remember that they have aspirations at all. This is the way of the Neo-Peasant: yes, he may have some rudimentary ambitions and dreams, amorphous and foggy though they may be, but he is just so *distracted* that it is impossible for him to focus any of these blurry images into sharp relief.

Categories of Vision

The Neo-Peasant is a blind man with no recognition of he *is;* no mental image of who he wants to *become;* and no sense of what *legacy* he wishes to build. The Neo-Peasant is he who has not implemented the Second Pillar of the Neo-Renaissance Man in his life: he may be materially rich, but without Vision, *he is creatively destitute.* As such, the three categories of Vision are:

- SELF-IMAGE: the Vision of who you *are,* now, this very moment.

- IMAGINATION: the Vision of who you want to *become,* in the future.

- LEGACY: the Vision of who you will "be" *after you have died.*

Transcending the "Mundane"

For the Neo-Renaissance Man, Vision paves the way for transcending the "mundane" responsibilities of life. All of life is not reducible to the grind of ensuring that various duties and errands are attended to. Responsibility is the First Pillar of the Neo-Renaissance Man because no higher endeavours may be adequately focused upon if basic chores and obligations are being pathologically ignored and avoided.

However, once one's responsibilities have been sufficiently honoured, a man inevitably begins to wonder if life has anything of more *substance* and *weight* to offer . . . he begins to feel the burn of AMBITION.

II. Vision

Vision is the blast furnace of aspiration: it is the mental space in which a man's Missions are forged, and the realm in which he discovers his deeper sense of Purpose. All great conquests were first achieved in the mind, within the creative faculty of the imagination. For the Neo-Renaissance Man, Vision is therefore the pathway to self-mastery and his own personal evolution because *Vision is the instrument that renders the mental ideal of that which he then takes action to materialize into concrete reality.*

i. Self-Image

"The human being always acts and feels and preforms in accordance with what he imagines to be true about himself and his environment ... We act, or fail, not because of 'will', as is so commonly believe, but because of imagination."

— Maxwell Maltz

Who are you, *right now*? The vision of the man who you *are* is what is called your SELF-IMAGE. This self-image has nothing to do with material goals or task-oriented accomplishment: it is a matter of *being*. Who are you, *now*, right this moment, as a man? What is your character? What sort of image are you projecting when you walk into a room? What kind of man do you see when you look into the mirror? To become a Neo-Renaissance Man, you must construct a detailed mental image of exactly the man who you *are*.

Psycho-Cybernetics

There was a plastic surgeon in the 1950's who wrote a book called *Psycho-Cybernetics* in which the concept of the self-image was developed. Dr. Maxwell Maltz's thesis was that a person's internally constructed self-image is a "guidance mechanism" that steers a person toward selecting the appropriate attitudes, actions and behaviours necessary to stay aligned with their subconscious conception of themselves.

II. Vision

"You will act," he summarized, "like the sort of person you conceive yourself to be." The power of the self-image to influence one's life is so magnificent that Dr. Maltz felt it was the psychological linchpin of success, achievement and happiness – or inversely, the ultimate cause of potential failure, defeatism and depression.

The self-image concept is therefore not to be interpreted as an abstract metaphor: *it is a very real psychological mechanism of the subconscious mind.* It exists and operates whether you are aware of it or not. As such, if you do not consciously program your self-image, and if you do not provide a clear vision of exactly the self-image that you wish to have, *your subconscious mind will rely upon the external environment for guidance in programming "who you are".*

Identity Slavery

If you do not consciously, deliberately create the vision of the man who you *are,* the media; advertiser; the government; critical associates; well meaning but unimaginative friends and family – *they*, collectively, will program your self-image for you. In this inertial age of comfort-worship, work-shirking, pathological avoidance of pain, and the veneration of entertainment as the *raison d'être* – in other words, in this epoch known as the Dark-Age of Decadence – *such suggestibility is self-evidently a very dangerous disposition to adopt.*

Remember: the Neo-Peasant did not create the Dark-Age of Decadence: this Neo-Dark Age created the Neo-Peasant. Why? Because the average man of this era fails to take responsibility for answering the question "Who am I?" ... *and therefore his external environment answers the question for him.* You must deliberately generate the vision of the man who you *are*, or else malevolent social influences may well do it for you – *and not to your advantage.*

The failure to assume responsibility for engineering your own self-image inevitably results in an insidious form of 'identity slavery'. Just as power abhors a vacuum, so too does the self-image: if you do not consciously provide the creative materiel that your subconscious requires to sculpt the self-image, foreign influences will hijack the process and create an identity that suites *their* objectives and purposes, not yours.

The result is the Neo-Peasant: men who are slaves to artificially implanted consumer, political or religious identities – pawns, in other words, that can be easily influenced and manipulated to serve the imperatives of those who control these identities. This is why consciously assuming control of cultivating your self-image is so imperative: *the alternative is psychological slavery.*

Self-Esteem

Of course, it could be argued that most men *do* actively participate in the programming of their own self-image: *whenever you think negatively about yourself you are unwittingly programming a correspondingly disparaging and destructive self-image.* The subconscious mind does not discriminate: it simply absorbs – like a spongy computer – all information that pertains to the query "Who Am I", regardless of the source, irrespective of the harmful nature of the data.

It is therefore your imperative responsibility to deliberately program a positive, constructive, confident self-image of the man you envision yourself to be. This is called cultivating healthy SELF-ESTEEM.

Having a positive self-image is not "egotistical" or "narcissistic". A psychologist named Nathaniel Brandon wrote a classic book called *The Six Pillars of Self-Esteem* in which he described the crucial role that a healthy sense of self-esteem plays in the development of your self-image. Brandon:

> *"When a man of self-esteem chooses his values and sets his goals, when he projects the long range purposes that will unify and guide his actions – it is like a bridge thrown to the future, across which his life will pass, a bridge supported by the conviction that his mind is competent to think, to judge, to value, and that he is worthy of enjoying values.*

In this passage not only does Brandon highlight the pivotal importance of self-esteem, but he also astutely ties the role of the self-image into the wider context of a man's life: *how can a man possibly commit to an ambitious mission if he does not first have the self-assurance that his vision of that pursuit is grounded in reality, rooted in a realistic self-assessment of his own capabilities?*

Without a healthy sense of self-esteem, a man's ability to connect with his creative faculty of Vision is crippled, and that disability ripples out and detrimentally influences all other aspects of his life, like a plague.

Creating an indomitable self-image does not mean lying to yourself and ignoring genuine weaknesses or limitations; nor does it involve selling yourself short by minimizing your true capacities. Rather, as Brandon himself put it, *"Self-esteem is the reputation we acquire with ourselves,"* and reputations are born out of reliable experience and honest, objective observation. You must learn to trust that the self-image you are consciously developing is genuinely *you;* only then may you unlock the latent power that is unleashed when you deliberately engineer your own self-image.

Becoming Who You *Are*

Becoming a Neo-Renaissance Man is not an event that is "achieved" in the future; it is not a task; nor is it a destination that is arrived at – *you become a Neo-Renaissance Man the instantaneous moment that you definitively decide to define yourself as such!*

You can transform from living the life of the Neo-Peasant, squabbling in the inertial excrement of your "Religion of Comfortableness", to living the life of the Noble Man, striving ever towards excellence, self-mastery and personal evolution, *instantly,* simply by authentically choosing to define yourself as such.

In the very moment that you decide to commit yourself to The Path of the Neo-Renaissance Man, even if you are simultaneously standing amidst the charred wreckage of your former life as a Neo-Peasant, *you are still nonetheless instantly transformed.* Your self-image is who you are NOW – not five years ago, not even five hours ago.

Always remember: it is your sovereign right as a man to change the Vision of who you are at any time, in any moment. *You become who you ARE.* Consider this statement carefully, for there is profound truth hidden behind its deceptive simplicity.

The Neo-Renaissance Man is he who purposefully generates a vivid vision of exactly the man whom he *is*. No matter what mistakes he made in the past and no matter the hardships he inevitably will face in the future, the Neo-Renaissance Man steadfastly persists in forging an indomitable self-image, tempering it daily in the creative flames of Vision. Most men could not answer the question: "Who are you" other than to mumble their name. The Neo-Renaissance Man, however, is he who can tell you in rich detail *exactly* who he is.

II. Vision

ii. Imagination

Who is the man whom you are destined to *become*? Who do you want to be by the time you are the elder statesman of the kingdom of your life? To answer this question you must employ the creative faculty of IMAGINATION: instrument of Vision, designer of dreams, and the mental forge of any concept of who you are to *become*.

Lack of Imagination is Fatal

It is all too typical of the Neo-Peasant to lack an inspiring vision of his own future. The average man of contemporary Western Civilization endeavours basically to be comfortable, safe, and perpetually stimulated by entertainment. If this archetypal avatar of the Dark-Age of Decadence has any "ambition" at all, it is simply to be *more* comfortable, *more* entertained, indulge in *more* of the extravagance of material consumption that our age has liberally made available.

There is no trace of the Neo-Renaissance Man's noble sense of vision in the consumer-oriented "ambitions" of the Neo-Peasant: it is just lazy consumption, a substitute for the vacuum that forms in a man when he does not nourish his spirit with a vision harvested from his own imagination.

The brute fact is that if you do not actively, consciously, deliberately take control of your creative faculty of imagination and direct it towards *envisioning exactly the man whom you desire to become*, then you will inevitably wilt and wither due to the sheer mediocrity of that comes to define your life, or otherwise implode – like a star that collapses upon itself after growing fat and useless – due to the gravity of your own lethargy.

Imagination, in the context of the Four Pillars of the Neo-Renaissance Man, is thus not a fuzzy, indeterminate concept presented to you with the intention of rousing a cheap emotional hit of "motivation"; it is not a soul-less "Self-Help" platitude; it is not a bumper sticker exhortation: the role of IMAGINATION in the Neo-Renaissance Man's life is that it facilitates the *deliberate visualization of the future he desires* – for a man cannot accomplish great deeds if he does not first *imagine* them.

It is true that imagination alone does not create reality: meditating in a cave does not forge empires – the shaman must eventually descend from the mountain to become the warrior-king – but imagination *does* produce the psychospheric space wherein the ephemeral spark of *action* can be manifested. When you mentally visualize whom you wish to become you begin spontaneously taking action in accordance with that Vision: *you become who you imagine yourself to be.*

Visualization

The art of mental visualization is therefore a paramount ritual practice (more on this in a later chapter) that the Neo-Renaissance Man must systematically implement into the daily routine of his life. Undistracted mental focus upon specific questions empowers your imagination to generate unique and creative answers.

Ask yourself, "Who do I wish to *become*," and then sit in quiet contemplation, focusing upon this question. Creative and relevant answers *will* bubble to the surface of your consciousness, their precise origins not always exactly known, but the value of these ideas and visions nonetheless self-evident.

Do not stress about clinging to any idea in particular. Allow the flow of your imagination to continue unabated. Simply observe your thoughts and allow your imagination to populate your mind with a panoramic patchwork of all that is possible. When you conclude your visualization session, rest assured: the ideas that are truly revolutionary *will not* be forgotten – they will have struck you with such force that you will not be able to shake them from your mind. You may even be left in a state of disbelief that you had never considered their possibility before. This is how you know you have stumbled upon a true *Vision*.

The inner-workings of the imagination are not entirely understood. In many ways, the faculty of imagination is the Mariana Trench of the mind: we may have some idea of what dwells on the surface, but the ocean depths of the subconscious remain an uncharted abyss. Your level of trust in the mysterious machinations of the imagination is directly proportional to the quality of creative solutions that it will yield, however.

Journaling

The medium of writing seems to produce qualitatively different creative results than purely mental visualization, just as the paint-brush produces different works of art than the hammer and chisel. The regular act of journaling, in conjunction with the aforementioned habit of mental visualization, is therefore also an essential practice for honing the definitive Vision of the man whom you desire to become.

As with the art of mental visualization, first ask the question, "Who do I wish to *become"*, and then pay close attention to the thoughts that flash into existence. This time, however, instead of silently witnessing as these ideas flit across your mind, *immediately write them down,* without prejudice, judgment or deliberation. Just write. The more automatic and indiscriminate you are in recording the ideas and inspirations generated by your imagination, the more you empower the unconscious source of your inspiration to produce a compelling vision of who you desire to become.

The act of writing is the first step in the material manifestation of your ambitions. When ideas are committed to the permanent seal of ink to paper; they are cemented into reality: no longer can you ignore your secret ambitions by suppressing them into the abyss of your subconscious – *they have become an objective reality that can no longer be denied.*

Vision Precedes Mission

The purpose of the faculty of imagination is not to concoct a fantasy that you lose yourself in: that is just another form of *distraction*. Imagination is the organic synthesizer of concrete goals: who do you want to become, what do you want to accomplish? *The spirit of any mission worth dedicating energy to is derivative of a corresponding vision that inspired it.*

If the goals and projects in your life do not motivate you toward taking definitive action – if they do not fill you with a sense of *mission* – it is probably because they are not products of your own imagination: you likely settled for these "goals", or were assigned them, or inherited them, but you certainly did not forge them in the kiln flames of your creative imagination. Without imaginative Vision, there is no goal, no target, no ambition – no primal desire to *become.*

All great empire builders are artists – no, *magicians* – for they all built their dynasties first within the inner-sanctum of their imagination before initiating even a single action toward the actual manifestation of their vision. The Neo-Renaissance Man is he who recognizes that Vision precedes Mission, and also that it is *imagination* that is the facilitator, the bridge, between these two great meta-principles of self-mastery and personal evolution.

iii. Legacy

"Man constantly makes his choice concerning the mass of present potentialities; which of these will be condemned to nonbeing and which will be actualized? Which choice will be made an actuality once and forever, an immortal 'footprint in the sands of time'? At any moment, man must decide, for better or for worse, what will be the monument of his existence."

— *Victor Frankl*

"What you do in life echoes in eternity."

— *Maximus Decimus Meridius (Gladiator, 2000)*

Who Will You "Be" After Death?

Who will you *be* after you have died? A seemingly paradoxical question, to be sure, as by definition death is the absence of "being". Yet, this question captures the essence of the word LEGACY: that which remains after a man has ceased to be.

To ask, *"What shall be my legacy?"* is to ask what the sum totality of your life accounts to after that great, final reconciliation occurs: death. What accomplishments did you achieve that you will be remembered for? What fortunes, material or otherwise, did you bequeath to your decedents? What impact did you have upon the universe itself? These are all matters concerning *legacy*.

II. Vision

Just as with the first two great questions which the Neo-Renaissance Man asks himself – "Who am I *now*", and "Who will I be *tomorrow*" – the question "Who will I be after *death*" is a question that explicitly pertains to the domain of Vision: *you must intentionally imagine exactly what your legacy will be in order to consciously conduct yourself in accordance with fulfilling that legacy.*

The Cosmic Ledger

It is the petty man of dim-witted vision who retorts, "But I'll be dead, who cares what my 'legacy' will be if I'm not there to appreciate it!" Legacy is not about your petty ego, though; it is not about *you;* your legacy is not *for* you. Matters of legacy are concerned, ultimately, with the notion that *what you do in life etches itself into the very fabric of the universe – irreversibly, irrevocably, and forever: nothing goes unrecorded in the cosmic ledger of eternity.*

A molecule of water that splashes into an ocean fundamentally alters the structure of the *entire* ocean. The water molecule, the instant that it hits the mass of water, immediately alters the condition of the other molecules that it physically hits. Those molecules, in turn, microscopically bounce and bump and gyrate into the molecules surrounding them, fundamentally altering *their* course as well – and so on, in a cause-and-effect wave that eventually cascades across the entire ocean. The influence that a drop of water has on the ocean as a whole is almost infinitely small, yes, but importantly it is theoretically measurable. *A single molecule of water leaves a legacy that changes the composition of the entire ocean.*

The Monument of your Existence

Your life, too, fundamentally leaves a very real imprint upon the universe. While your actions may seem insignificant when compared to the macroscopic scale of the universe – just like a molecule of water dropped into an ocean – *the legacy of your life nonetheless splashes into the ocean of time and its influence inevitably ripples across the cosmic ether.*

Who can know what influence our lives truly have upon the universal pulse of existence – only the gods. But do recognize that your life *does* indeed leave an imprint upon the universe that can never be erased. A man's actions will forever stand as a "monument of his existence," as psychologist Viktor Frankl put it. *A man's legacy is truly and literally eternal.*

When considered from this perspective, matters of legacy inherit an existential gravity: building a worthy legacy is not about attempting to 'avoid death', like filmmaker Woody Allen implied when he said, "I don't want to achieve immortality through my works; I want to achieve immortality by not dying." *To envision your legacy is to decide what images will be permanently captured on the cosmic filmstrip of universal history.*

It is only the archetype of the Neo-Renaissance Man who considers his existence from such cosmic perspectives. In order to approach greatness you must first adopt great perspective. Envisioning your legacy is about stretching the boundaries of your imagination beyond the limits of your own mortal perceptions.

Think cosmically: *"What thunderous symphony of a life shall I orchestrate? What euphonious legacy shall I broadcast into the reverberating matrix of the universe, destined to echo through the great halls of infinite?* Choose to think small and you shall

II. Vision

live a small life; consider your life from the perspective of the eternal, and you shall live greatly.

"Who will I *be* when I am dead," the Neo-Renaissance Man ponders. Indeed: what will *your* legacy be? Will it be that you lived an average, safe, comfortable life? Shall that be the "monument of your existence", a little pile of rocks camouflaged amidst an ocean of stones? *Or shall your life be a great monolith that silhouettes shapely against the horizon, casting long shadows upon the scattered piles of rocks surrounding it?*

Legacy Inspires Desire

The practical role that this practice of envisioning your legacy serves is to inspire intense, burning DESIRE – the sort that inspires action, justifies sacrifice, and demands perseverance. To conjure vivid images of your legacy from the perspective of the eternal will provide the impetus to commit to great endeavours *today*. By imagining your legacy from the perspective of eternity you give yourself permission to envision your goals, aspirations, and desires without confining your sense of vision to the limited duration of your life.

The Perspective of Eternity

An empire's legacy is that which remains after the empire's inevitable collapse: it is the *eternal spirit* of the culture. Greco-Roman civilization, for example, has long since disintegrated, yet the Greco-Roman *spirit* was revived during the Renaissance and continues to live vicariously within the soul of the West.

So be it with your life, as well: long after you have died, *may your legacy become legend*. Build the empire of your life, and do not despair that it shall inevitably disintegrate, *for your legacy shall be permanent in ways that you do not – indeed, cannot – understand.* "What shall be my legacy?" Ask yourself this question daily. Envision who you intend to become in this life in such vivid detail that you even imagine who you will "be" long after you have joined your ancestors.

The culture of the Dark-Age of Decadence is fundamentally one of short attention spans and even shorter measures of what is considered "long-term". The average man does not even know what he is going to do *tomorrow,* let alone what his *eternal legacy* shall be. The Neo-Renaissance Man is he who adopts the perspective of eternity when envisioning the legacy of his life, and it is perhaps this perspective that is the true wellspring of his overflowing sense of nobility.

II. Vision

Conclusion

The operative role of Vision in the life of the archetypical Neo-Renaissance Man is to generate the *desire* that he then uses to orient and fuel his *action*. Weak desire yields weak results, just as a tiny fire produces insignificant heat. You can have no definitive sense of Mission and serve no meaningful Purpose in life if you harbour a murky sense of Vision. It is Vision that is the generator of motivation and the fountainhead of energy. *Vision is the spark that ignites action.* Indeed, Vision is the metaphysical bridge between abstract creative imagination and concrete MISSION.

The Third Pillar of the Neo-Renaissance Man:

Mission

MISSONS are conceived in the subjective womb of intangible imagination. However, once a Mission has been firmly established and committed to, it then becomes grounded in reality, no longer a dream, but a logistical operation. *The war begins:* bearings and waypoints are plotted; objectives are defined; deadlines are committed to; and most fundamentally, *action* is initiated. MISSION is the process of transforming abstract Vision into concrete reality through the initiation of objective action.

Failure & Defeat

Missions are by nature achievable through the successful fulfillment of specific objectives, and therefore the prospect of *failure* also becomes a distinct possibility. The encounter of significant obstacles to the accomplishment of a challenging mission is not a probability, but a guarantee. "No plan survives contact with the enemy," the soldier reminds himself.

Persistence and resilience are required to continue the assault towards the accomplishment of your missions in the face of resistance, and even then failures will still occur. Recognize, though, that "failure" is merely a counter-attack that may be parried; failure only becomes *defeat* when you stop fighting and surrender the cause.

On "Closure"

With sufficient tenacity though, success shall inevitably be realized in the pursuit of your missions. The trap that many men subsequently fall prey to, however, is that they simply *stop* and commit to no subsequent challenges; they "rest on their laurels". *For the average man, success is poison because they confuse it for 'closure'.*

This is one of the fatal mistakes that the Neo-Peasant makes if he ever happens upon some measure of success in his life, accidental or otherwise. Success is fatal to those who mistake it for a signal that they may reasonably cease to embrace the mission-oriented life. *Every man needs a mission, always.*

The Neo-Renaissance Man is he who is never without a mission: when his greatest conquest is achieved, he dusts himself off, takes a moment to savour the victory, and then immediately embarks upon establishing a new noble war to hurl himself into. Individual campaigns may end, but the Third Pillar of the Neo-Renaissance Man, *Mission*, is eternal.

III. Mission

Categories of Mission

For the Neo-Renaissance Man there are three types of Mission:

- ARCH-MISSIONS: the defining missions of your life. There will only a few of them, maybe even just one, throughout the duration of your life.

- TERTIARY: the multitude of subordinate goals and projects that you commit to in parallel to your Arch-Mission.

- RITUALS & RESOLUTIONS: constitute a special category of Mission, for they do not have any "end-state" that is ever arrived at. Like the practice of meditation, these missions never really end; there are merely periods of interlude between their practice.

Collectively, these three categories of Mission constitute the definitive course of action that the Neo-Renaissance Man organizes his life around, after ensuring that his responsibilities have been appropriately acknowledged and acted upon. Your Missions are your *war,* and they are waged as such: they are well-planned, actionable operations, not abstract dreams or incoherent desires.

Without Mission, a man's life is an empty shell. Life sinks into drudgery. The Third Pillar of the Neo-Renaissance Man elevates a man's existence to the mode of the action-oriented warrior, an archetype that is unknown to the Neo-Peasant who fails or otherwise refuses to become a *Man of Action.*

i. Arch-Mission

An organized, motivated man can accomplish more before seven in the morning than the average man accomplishes in an entire day: *imagine what such a man can accomplish with the same focused, sustained action over the course of years, decades, or a lifetime?*

Your Crusade

Your Arch-Mission is the Great Work of your life. Given the extensive scope and extended timeframes associated with Arch-Missions, however, it is imperative that a man possess a burning desire to succeed, for any weakness of resolve will inevitably result in an abandoning of the campaign. An Arch-Mission is not a hobby, nor an idle fantasy: it is an all-out *crusade* that will in many ways come to define your legacy. As such, your commitment to your Arch-Mission must be fanatical in nature.

Sacrifice & Austerity

The concept of the Arch-Mission is antithetical to the culture of the Dark-Age of Decadence, in which instant gratification, passive entertainment, and avoidance of pain or suffering are so ubiquitous so as to be considered self-evident virtues and sacred values. As such, there are so few men who ever commit to concrete Arch-Missions in life – due to the sacrifice of comfort and ease that it would require – *that the Neo-Renaissance Man's focused*

III. Mission

commitment to his Arch-Mission produces a jarring, disorienting contrast.

For the archetype of the average man of our epoch, the Neo-Peasant, the hope of even *knowing* what their Arch-Mission is, let alone accomplishing it, is dim: they are just too distracted; too inundated by the all-out assault on their senses by omnipresent media screens; too paralyzed by their avoidance of life's responsibilities; too blinded by their lack of vision. To commit to a genuine Arch-Mission, for the typical Neo-Peasant, is entirely out of the realm of possibility due to the sheer level of commitment and dedication that Arch-Missions require.

Commitment to the accomplishment of your chosen Arch-Mission *will* require the implementation of a policy of AUSTERITY in your life. Do not gloss over this fact: definitive commitment to your Arch-Mission will require sacrifices that you cannot currently imagine or foresee. Arch-Missions are *wars*, and a primeval fog of war hangs thick in the context of any such protracted campaign: be prepared to encounter heavy resistance that you cannot presently anticipate or prepare for. All that can be done is to advance toward your objective and adapt to the situation when you inevitably come into contact with resistance to the accomplishment of your Arch-Mission.

Conversely though, the Great Mission of your life that you may have been habitually postponing, perhaps for years, might not be as daunting as your imagination has estimated. It could be that your Arch-Mission is so well suited to your capabilities and so compatible with your temperament that its accomplishment is achieved at an almost magical speed once you finally commit to sustained action. *The only reason it took so long to achieve success is that it took you so long to definitively commit to the Mission.*

Your Arch-Mission may require crawling in the trenches and grinding away for years before victory is achieved, yes – *but the war might also be won so swiftly that the speed of the conquest comes as a shock even to yourself.* All that was every holding you back was *you*.

Mastery & Creation

How does a man decide upon what his chosen Arch-Mission shall be? There are a few parameters that the Neo-Renaissance Man uses as basic guidelines. An Arch-Mission should be a goal that involves either the development of a skill to a high degree of mastery or the production of a valuable creative product. Considered from the negative perspective, what an Arch-Mission *should not* encompass is the mere acquisition of material possessions.

For example, it is not the way of the Neo-Renaissance Man to select as his Arch-Mission the attainment of, say, an extravagant mansion. There is no *skill* involved in this goal; no sense of development – no aspect of personal evolution or self-mastery. It is just the empty goal of acquiring a big house. *If a man is to have a mansion, let it be an ancillary prize for the mastering of a skill or the creation of a product of great value.*

Consider such material rewards as incidental bonuses that sometimes happen to coincide with the pursuit and achievement of your Arch-Mission, *but which are never pursued for their own sake.* The Neo-Renaissance Man is he who is committed to self-mastery and personal evolution, and his definitive mission in life should suitably reflect these values rather than mere materialistic acquisition for its own sake.

The Boy Within

Another guideline for selecting an appropriate Arch-Mission to commit to: reflect upon your boyhood reveries, dreams, and aspirations. Often the "boy within" is the silent keeper of your purest, most unadulterated aspirations. If you analyze your boyhood memories carefully, you should discover certain unifying threads and recurring themes that may be translated into tangible, objective Arch-Missions in adulthood.

You may well have forgotten these keys to your sense of noble ambition during the inevitable transition from childhood to adolescence and then finally into adulthood, but your "boy within" did not. Reconnect with that uncorrupted boyhood vision and you may discover that you have known what your definitive mission in life was supposed to be all along.

The Colossus of Your Life

Regardless of the details and origins of your Arch-Mission, what is imperative is that you do indeed have a definitive project, a master mission, a Great Work that you have definitively committed to. Maintaining an array of Tertiary Missions to compliment your superordinate Arch-Mission is important (for reasons that shall be explored in the next chapter), but to have *only* these comparatively limited goals and projects – to the exclusion of a master goal – would be to cheat yourself of the exaltation and triumph of great, hard-fought victories.

To your dying die, you shall, you *must* have a definitive mission to commit yourself to. And even once victory has been attained, even after your empire has been built and is flourishing, *you must then begin preparations for your next Great Mission!*

The mission-oriented nature of the Neo-Renaissance Man only rests in the eternal slumber of death. Serious dedication to an Arch-Mission is what separates the Neo-Renaissance Man from the Neo-Peasant who merely drifts through life, what accomplishments he does achieve occurring by accident or through sheer happenstance, like a promotion "awarded" due to seniority.

Without a central Arch-Mission to centre yourself upon, your life will come to resemble urban sprawl: stretched-out and without centrality; spiritually void; an endless vista of gray mediocrity. No, let your Arch-Mission be the Colossus of your life, *upon which all else is patterned, upon which all of your other accomplishments and achievements gaze upwards in awe!*

Mission & Purpose

A final word on discovering the Arch-Mission of your life, and a preview of what is to follow in this book: look to your *Purpose* for inspiration. Vision, the Second Pillar of the Neo-Renaissance Man, will conjure a vivid mental construct of exactly what you wish to accomplish, but it may well be Purpose that provides the original impetus for the vision of what your Great Project shall be. More on this subject shall be revealed later, but keep this in mind when considering what the nature of your Arch-Mission will be.

What would the archetype of the Neo-Renaissance Man be without a definitive Arch-Mission guiding his most focused and intense energies? It almost goes without saying that *of course* the Neo-Renaissance Man is perpetually engaging with a serious, complex, difficult mission. To "live" without a Great Mission is merely to biologically exist without purpose.

Karmic Gravity

It is a serious dereliction of your sacred duty as a man to shirk the undertaking of such personal crusades in life. You are *alive*, during a span of time that amounts to a speck of dust suspended above the cavernous abyss of Non-Being: you were not given this one chance at life as a man to merely live a safe, comfortable, "sufficiently entertained" existence. You have been blessed with this *one chance* to accomplish something great, whatever that may be, in whatever form it may take.

Napoleon Hill, a pioneer of the field that he entitled "the Philosophy of Achievement", wrote about a period of his life when he had been persistently neglecting his Arch-Mission, which was to write a book detailing the principles of achievement and success. Hill recounts how one evening, as he continued to procrastinate and avoid working on his book, he had a sudden flash of intuition, and a voice told him this:

> *"Your mission in life: if you neglect it, for any cause whatsoever, you will be reduced to a primal state and be forced to retrace the cycles [of your existence] which you have passed during thousands of years."*

A chilling, sobering passage, for the Neo-Renaissance Man, and a warning: do not neglect the necessity of selecting and pursuing an Arch-Mission in life, *for perhaps the consequences for failing to do so are graver than you can possibly conceive.* You are the legacy of thousands of generations of your sacred ancestors who came before you; you are the bleeding edge; the tip of the spear; the only living conduit of your lineage capable of preserving the integrity and honour of your heritage — so act like it, and *go to war!* Honour your ancestors by pursuing an Arch-Mission worthy of their legacy.

ii. Tertiary Missions

Every Neo-Renaissance Man engages with a battery of goals and projects concurrent with but unrelated to his Arch-Mission. These are called TERTIARY MISSIONS: creative projects and constructive hobbies that enrich your life, as well as the practice of goal setting and systematic tracking of progress.

Tertiary Missions provide *structure* to the "spare-time" that a man inevitably finds in his life so that he does not easily fall prey to the passive amusements and idle entertainment that proliferate in this Dark-Age of Decadence. For the Neo-Renaissance Man, Tertiary Missions provide an opportunity to continue pursuing self-mastery and personal evolution even during the compulsorily "down-time" from attending to the serious work related to his Arch-Mission, *but in such a way that he does not exhaust himself.*

Killing Time

The pursuit of Tertiary Missions transforms what used to be blocks of time wasted on passive entertainment into regenerative and creative relaxation. The Neo-Renaissance Man does not "relax" by watching television for six hours a day, like the Neo-Peasant: he relaxes by pursuing a lifelong program of auto-didacticism, skill-based hobbies, and difficult but enjoyable challenges.

Men of this age always seem to want to "kill time", especially those little blocks of time where *supposedly* nothing of value may be accomplished. The Neo-Peasant is he who is bathed in the blood of such wasted time, despite having access to productivity enhancing technology that *should* have made him the *most* productive man, ever.

What can you accomplish in fifteen minutes? In this Dark-Age of Decadence, fifteen-minute blocks of spare time are treated like a disease that must be eradicated. When the average man has fifteen spare minutes he typically squanders the potential of that time by staring, tapping, and flicking at his phone. The unholy rise of infinite scrolling social media has obliterated more small, *but potentially productive,* packets of time than any other technology in human history.

Harvesting Time

The Neo-Renaissance Man recognizes the power of one percent, however: you see, fifteen minutes is very close to being exactly one percent of a day. What can be accomplished with one percent of the day's time? With appropriate concentration, that tiny increment of time may be leveraged to: learn a language; sharpen your mathematics aptitude; study an interesting historical era; teach yourself how to read financial statements – only your curiosity limits you.

Nearly one hundred hours of focused study a year can be liberated from the mass of wasted time in our lives just by committing to effectively utilizing fifteen minutes a day rather than wasting it. Tertiary Missions provide an excellent opportunity for capitalizing on all those chunks of time that otherwise cannot be used for the accomplishment of more complex projects. Tertiary Missions allow you to *harvest* time, rather than *kill* time.

III. Mission

One of the great missed opportunities of our age is the ability to be educated while stuck in traffic, for example. If a man spends one hour a day in traffic, that represents *hundreds of hours a year* that may be allocated to autodidacticism through the medium of audiobooks. The time cannot be used for any other purpose anyways; it is wasted otherwise, so there is literally nothing to lose.

You can receive the equivalent of several university degrees worth of knowledge concerning a diverse array of subjects and disciplines over the course of a lifetime simply by better leveraging time that is otherwise wasted. Create a curriculum for yourself. It is within the context of Tertiary Missions that the framework for intentionally organizing such programs of enrichment and learning is facilitated.

Constructive Relaxation

Of course, there are some Tertiary Missions that will be more complex in nature. They may require blocks of several hours to be reserved for their activity. However, what separates *these* more complex Tertiary Missions from your Arch-Mission is that they are not driven by the same sense of fanatical necessity that is characteristic of your Arch-Missions.

Becoming, say, an excellent recreational tennis player certainly qualifies itself as a respectable Tertiary Mission that will require considerable focus and time, *but it is also probably not the driving ambition of your life*; you would not prioritize this project over your all-important Arch Mission. Rather, this sort of recreational project serves the objective purpose of providing a constructive mental break from your more pressing responsibilities and most serious goals.

Such projects are not passive, however. They still involve the mastery of skills and the application of creativity. You *engage* with your hobbies and personal projects, you *create*, unlike with the passive "activity" of watching television. Ultimately however, these projects are not meant to frustrate or exhaust: their purpose is to provide *regenerative relaxation* from the stressful responsibilities of life as well as from the serious work related to your Arch-Mission.

Goals & Objectives

The domain of Tertiary Missions is also the natural jurisdiction of the general practice of GOAL SETTING. Fitness standards, financial benchmarks, personal ambitions and every other kind of "check-box" goal are included in this category.

Goal setting provides useful metrics for the measurement of progress. More than anything, setting goals and tracking progress provides valuable, objective feedback that you remain "on the path" and that no significant course corrections are required.

If, however, a man observes empirical evidence that, say, his strength progression has been plateauing, or that his financial balance sheet has been declining in value, he is strategically positioned to react *rationally* and adjust his strategy and plans accordingly. He has access to *objective information* with which to base these decisions upon, as he has diligently tracked his progress against predetermined benchmarks.

This is why setting goals and tracking progress is so important; this is why Tertiary Missions play a pivotal role in the Neo-Renaissance Man's life, even if they are subordinate to his Arch-Missions: *self-mastery and personal evolution are not possible if progression and achievement is not measurable.*

Goals, objectives, benchmarks and personal records are not *intrinsically* important; they are essentially arbitrary and relative. What matters is the *behavioural influence* that the goal setting process and the practice of tracking progress have on a man.

When the Neo-Renaissance Man begins to objectively measure his personal evolution, in whatever contexts of his life, he will find that his performance is amplified and results are more forthcoming. The act of observation itself has a qualitative influence upon outcomes.

Improvement

It always comes back to this central orientation of the Neo-Renaissance Man: *continuous improvement.* In different ways, all Four Pillars of the Neo-Renaissance Man support this overarching thrust toward self-mastery. Tertiary Missions are no different: they may not be the prime focus of a man's life, but they serve his personal evolution by providing an outlet for relaxation *without resort to the hedonistic obliteration of higher-consciousness that the Neo-Peasant resorts to when he subsumes himself into the myriad distractions of this Dark Age of Decadence.*

This is the true role that Tertiary Missions play in the Neo-Renaissance Man's life: providing structure and direction to the entire context of your life – even "downtime" – *so that passivity and idleness cannot slither in and infect you with their poisons.*

iii. Rituals & Resolutions

The third categorical type of Mission for the Neo-Renaissance Man is RITUALS AND RESOLUTIONS. The committed adoption of Rituals and Resolutions as an integral component of your program of self-mastery will further temper your shield against the insidious influences, detours and moral corruption of this Dark-Age of Decadence.

Habit is Destiny

This final category of the Third Pillar of the Neo-Renaissance Man is fundamentally related to the phenomenon of HABIT. All men have habits, *but it is the Neo-Renaissance Man who consciously assumes control of the habit-forming process and decides exactly which habits he will nourish . . . and which he shall eradicate.*

The purpose of Rituals and Resolutions are to create an array of simple routines that are integrated into your daily life. The objective is for these practices to become so automatic, so *habitual,* that accomplishing them does not require energy or concentration. Few people feel that brushing their teeth is a burdensome use of five minutes of their day: indeed, you do not plan for this activity, nor schedule it; you do not even think about it – you just ritualistically brush your teeth, no matter how busy life is. This is the goal of Rituals and Resolutions: *to encourage the formation of positive habits that become seamless extensions of your personality.*

III. Mission

Who is the Neo-Peasant? He is the average man of our decadent age whose life is dominated by *habit,* as is the life of the Neo-Renaissance Man. However, the distinction is that *the Neo-Peasant makes little or no effort to consciously choose which habits he nurtures, and which he wills to abolish.*

In fact, the Neo-Peasant is not even aware of many of his most destructive habitual tendencies: they have burrowed deeply into the fabric of his daily routine, and his sense of self-awareness has atrophied due to being perpetually bombarded by all the distractions and diversions of this Dark-Age of Decadence.

The double-edge blade of habit cuts in both directions: habits will either ennoble a man or otherwise destroy him. If you, now or in the past, have been living the spiritually destitute life of a Neo-Peasant, ask yourself: *in what ways do your habits affect the totality of who you are?* How will they influence who you will be a decade from now if they continue to persist? What will your habits have made of you by the end of your life? *Habit is destiny* . . . for better or for worse.

So much that dooms the archetype of the Neo-Peasant to being so characteristically irresponsible, so visionless, so lacking in ambition is linked to the absence of self-awareness in regards to the habits that collectively drive much of his behaviour. Sometimes it is the subtle differences that divide the "common" from the "great". The Neo-Renaissance Man's simple commitment to assuming conscious control of the phenomenon of habit is one of those finer differences.

If all a man were to do was to endeavour to be the discerning curator of his own habits, even if he otherwise declined to undertake any other type of grander mission in his life, this act alone would still revolutionize his life.

Rituals

RITUALS are task-oriented missions that, by their very nature, are easily convertible into *habits*. Some Missions – such as your Arch and Tertiary Missions – are complex and non-linear; they usually require logistical planning, abstract problem solving, and sometimes large, dense blocks of time dedicated to them. *These types of missions cannot typically be routinized and converted into habits.* Rituals, however, can easily be converted into habits because the activity involved in ritualized pursuits is usually simple, linear, and automatable.

Eternal Missions

Herein is revealed an essential characteristic of the Ritual Mission: rituals are, by their very nature, never *completed;* there is no closure; no accomplishment – there is only the interlude from one ritual session to the next, like the harmonic silence between music notes that are actually *a part* of the symphony rather than the absence of it.

Ritual Missions, by definition, are essentially non-achievable, and this is one of the major reasons why they are categorized separately from the task-oriented Arch and Tertiary Missions. One never "accomplishes" the Ritual Mission of meditation, for example: the ritual of meditation is a mission that never ends. You can become more skilled and proficient at meditation, move from adept to master, *but this is never achieved by doing anything other than sitting down and meditating.* No grand strategy is

III. Mission

required, only discipline, *and once rituals have become ingrained habits, not even discipline is required.*

The practical benefit of ritual practices is that they liberate mental energy because they have the almost magical tendency to schedule themselves into your routine once they become habitual. Rituals fill in the little cracks of time scattered throughout the day that go otherwise wasted; they naturally dwell in the intermissions between large, time-consuming projects – time that often would otherwise be wasted.

The ultimate objective of Ritual Missions is to reach a level of unconscious routine in which the necessity of *discipline* is eliminated altogether: you want your rituals to become so automatic, so habitual, that whenever circumstances render their practice temperately impossible, you feel naked and unsettled. Your rituals should eventually be so strongly grooved into the pattern of your routine that it would take intense discipline *not* to practice them.

Resolutions

So what then is RESOLUTION in the context of the Third Pillar of the Neo-Renaissance Man? Resolutions are commitments, binding contracts, *promises* that you make to yourself *not* to do something, but which you approach from a mission-oriented perspective: you make it an *objective* to respect your resolutions. The purpose of your resolutions, in other words, is to shatter the "bad habits" in your life, or prevent them from taking root in the first place.

Anti-Habits

Another way to view this sub-categorical type of Mission is to recognize resolutions as being *anti-habits*. Your resolutions are your great, personally dictated *Thou Shalt Not's*. They are self-demarcated boundaries and rules. They initially require discipline, for if you had to resolve *not* to do a particular activity or action, it is likely because you have already struggled with self-control in relation to that context.

Indeed, the breaking of your most deeply rooted "bad habits" may prove to be extraordinarily difficult. Some of your specific resolutions may represent the most difficult undertaking you have ever committed to, potentially. This is why they are classified as Missions: you must have a zealous, militant, mission-oriented attitude toward respecting the resolutions that you commit to.

The Neo-Peasant archetype is fatally characterized by a failure of self-discipline. This is another area in which the Neo-

Peasant is self-evidently the foil of the Neo-Renaissance Man, and is why the nature of the Neo-Peasant is analyzed so thoroughly in this book: he serves as a mirror in which we are forced to reflect upon those hidden aspects of ourselves that we may prefer not to identify.

For many men, their lack of willingness to reflect upon their weaknesses and "bad habits" ultimately culminates in an unconscious capitulation to the enemies of every sovereign man of this age: distraction, comfort and luxury – the "Religion of Comfortableness".

Instead, they stop resisting these temptations of the Dark-Age of Decadence and allow themselves to be definitively subsumed into a quagmire of their unchecked, unrestrained vices. The Neo-Peasant's failure to lead a resolute, disciplined life allows his unacknowledged self-destructive habits to fester, metastasize, and eventually to cannibalize him.

The Neo-Renaissance Man recognizes that the discipline of *resolution* must be treated like a sacred Mission. When a habit is recognized as blocking him from the full realization of his potential for self-mastery and personal evolution, the Neo-Renaissance Man resolves to obliterate that habit, "with extreme prejudice".

Resolutions are negative-missions, as it were: the inverse of action; the achievement of *not* engaging in a harmful activity or behaviour. Sometimes the greatest victory achieved in a war is to have *not* engaged in a certain battle.

Addiction

What are the habitual actions, routines, and yes, indeed, *addictions* in your life that are dragging you down from the rarefied air of the mountains in which self-mastery is pursued by the Neo-Renaissance Man and into the damp, drizzly gully of laziness, avoidance and perpetual distraction that the Neo-Peasant languishes in? Take a moment for self-reflection and consider this question seriously.

If you struggle with taking responsibility, connecting with your sense of vision, or with committing to a mission-oriented lifestyle, then perhaps the root blockage is not a failure to dedicate yourself to any of the above, *but rather is an addiction that has come to dominate your life.*

If this is the case, then your Mission, *your only mission*, is that of RESOLUTION: you must resolve to liberate yourself from the destructive compulsions that dominate your life. If you have been "hopelessly" stuck in the quicksand of your destructive habits and addictions, living like a miserable Neo-Peasant, then you know – yes, *you know* – what must be done.

The ignoble carnival distractions of the Dark-Age of Decadence are wonderfully effective at allowing you to anesthetise yourself from the reality of your problems, but eventually, inevitably, you must face the Neo-Peasant who gazes back at you in the mirror. Eventually, you must become *resolute* and seize control of your sovereignty from the tyranny of your compulsions.

III. Mission

Conclusion

A man without self-imposed objectives and goals is merely a biological male, for implicit in the eternal ideal of masculinity is serious dedication to MISSION. Interestingly, while there are legions of Western males who lack any masculine mission orientation at all, it would be almost impossible to find a boy who does not harbour a natural, healthy, inborn instinct driving him toward pursuing *Mission*.

From Boy to Warrior-King

A boy always has a mission, and this reveals itself in the games that he plays and through the vivid imagination that inspires his quests and crusades. The boy embraces the archetypes of the hero and the knight; he plays out the role of explorer and conquer – but most of all he eagerly anticipates becoming *king*, one day, when he becomes a man.

Always, for the boy, this pure and uncorrupted vision of himself as a *man* never has anything to do with living a safe, comfortable life of luxury filled with passive amusements and entertainment. Always, for the boy, he imagines himself as growing-up to be a *Man of Action*. If he sees himself as King, it is because the greatest nobility is discovered in the pursuit of the greatest missions.

You have been granted this one opportunity to be a *man*. Not long ago, you were born. Soon, you shall die. In the interlude between that mysterious state of Non-Being that bookends life, you have been granted this fleeting spark of time with which to test your mettle as a man on the battlefield of life.

You have parachuted into enemy lines: supplies are limited, you are surrounded, and you are greatly outnumbered – death is inevitable. But do not crawl into a hole and cower, waiting for the inevitable! Do not sell your life cheaply. You have a *Mission*. Bring the fight to the enemy; wreck havoc behind their lines; be a banshee of fanatical resistance in the face of inevitable death.

You shall die and all that you accomplish will soon after crumble into dust. What of it? Let your noble pursuit of Mission, the Third Pillar of the Neo-Renaissance Man, serve as the sort of smirking, death-defying laughter that could only possibly emanate from true men facing impossible odds.

The Fourth Pillar of the Neo-Renaissance Man:

Purpose

IN the 1950's a curious book titled *The Phenomenon of Man* was quietly published. The writer, a Jesuit priest, Pierre Teilhard de Chardin, presented a unique perspective concerning the fundamental nature of evolution. Teilhard argued that the phenomenon of evolution is actually "pulled" by a mysterious force dwelling in the future, rather than being "pushed towards" from the past, as is commonly conceived.

The Omega-Point

All of evolution is actually driven by the attraction to a 'transcendental object', a singularity at the end of time — or as Teilhard called it, the OMEGA-POINT. All history, all progress, all evolution, Teilhard argued, is attracted to this ontological singularity. It is this all-powerful metaphysical attractor in the future that is the ultimate driving force, the supreme motivator, and the cosmic generator of *purpose* in the universe, according to Teilhard.

PURPOSE is the Forth Pillar of the Neo-Renaissance Man: it is his sacred Omega-Point. He is attracted toward and *pulled* by this force; he does not *push* toward it like he does with his Missions. Purpose is not an objective to be achieved; it is not a series of tasks that, if accomplished, results in a state of finality.

Purpose is a path that never ends; it is eternal – a way of life. *Purpose, for the Neo-Renaissance Man, is a permanent orientation toward your own personal Omega-Point.* You can never definitively "achieve" the metaphysical object of your Purpose; rather, you are eternally guided by and attracted toward it.

Purpose can and will manifest itself in the *form* of Mission, *but the accomplishment of purpose inspired missions does not constitute the "completion" of Purpose.* The divine pulse of Purpose is forever pumping the oxygen rich blood of meaning and passion into your life. Purpose provides guidance for action, an impetus for it – a *raison d'être*.

Without Purpose, without the *meaning* provided by the Omega-Point of Purpose, there would be no reason to choose one otherwise arbitrary Vision for your life over another, and all prospective Missions would grey and atrophy soon after they were launched.

Destiny, Not Fate

Purpose is indeed destiny – *but it is not fate*. Fate is that which must happen, no matter what actions you take. Your fate is to die, for example, because it is an eventuality that is unavoidable. However, your Purpose is not your fate because it requires that you *choose* to follow its path; it requires commitment, discipline and resiliency:

IV. Purpose

it is not automatic – *it is not fate*. Purpose is a beacon that guides the ship of your life in the black fog of night, *but you must still steer the ship!*

The Neo-Renaissance Man is the *Man of Destiny*, and his counter-part, his foil, the Neo-Peasant, is the *Man of Fate*. The Neo-Renaissance Man is guided by Purpose, and takes responsibility for actually *living* that purpose, even when it calls for great sacrifice and austerity. The Neo-Peasant has no magnetic sense of purpose at all; his apparent "Omega-Point" is only whatever nifty distraction happens to beacon him in the whim of the moment.

The Neo-Peasant is truly the Man of Fate, for the course of his entire life is guided by a compass that is spinning madly due to the literal electromagnetic storm of distractions that cloud his life, unable to settle on a steady bearing toward his own personal True North. One of the tragedies of the Dark-Age of Decadence is that, amidst this kaleidoscopic storm of distractors that has come to define our historical epoch, most men never recognize what their purpose is to begin with, let alone properly orient their lives toward it.

Many men are not aware of what their purpose is because they have never stopped for a moment to consider the subject in quiet contemplation. If they were to be held captive in a monastery for a few weeks, with nothing to do but listen to monks chanting from dawn to dusk, *they would come to know their purpose*. The Neo-Renaissance Man is quintessentially the man who has gone through that process of austere contemplation and come to *know* his purpose.

Categories of Purpose

There are three types of Purpose for the Neo-Renaissance Man:

- YOUR GIFT: the exercise and development of your natural talents and abilities.

- PERSONAL MYTHOLOGY: the internalization of personally selected mythological stories, allegories and parables that provide essential narratives of meaning and purpose in your life.

- META-PURPOSE: there is one unifying Purpose that all Neo-Renaissance Men subscribe to and to which all other "purpose" is subordinate.

You must consciously orient your life toward that great metaphysical attractor, your Omega-Point, your *Purpose*. Do not surrender the responsibility of discovering your purpose to the capricious winds of fate. Assume total responsibility for discovering and pursuing your deepest purpose, your personal Omega-Point. Be a *Man of Destiny*: dedicate yourself to the Forth Pillar of the Neo-Renaissance Man and follow the guiding star of *your* Purpose.

IV. Purpose

i. Your Gift

YOUR GIFT is your purpose. Your gift is that which comes easily to you, but which for most people is difficult. Your gift is a skill or ability that you, perhaps from early childhood, were observed as being "a natural" at. Pursuit of the development of these natural talents is one of the central purposes of your life. *Mastery* of your gift is your purpose – indeed, it is your sacred duty. If you are in search of a definitive Arch-Mission to dedicate your life to, there is surely no better candidate than to pursue the mastery of your natural talents.

Mastery Is Never "Achieved"

Mastery of your gift is more related to Purpose than to Mission because missions, by definition, *end:* their objectives are completed; their vision is realized; they are fundamentally achieved – *but Purpose never ends*, and your gift, whatever it may be, does not expire when particular goals that it inspired are accomplished. Rather, your gift simply generates a *new* mission related to its own development.

Great artists do not retire; their work is merely interrupted by the imposition of death. This is because their work is not a "job", nor an idle hobby: it is their passion, their purpose – *their gift*. Projects related to your gift may be approached from the objective-orientated framework of Mission, *but the generative source that inspires these undertakings, Purpose, never ceases to produce fresh challenges and renewed objectives*. There are no limits to the progression of your skills, no caps to your level of mastery. *Evolution is forever.*

Mastery Is Not "Fun"

Whatever skills you excel at you are likely to be passionate about. A stallion is naturally passionate about galloping and he is said to be *"born to run"*. This is why it is so important to develop your gifts: it provides a vigorous sense of passion because you are doing what you naturally excel at.

However, passion is not to be confused with "entertainment". Making the development of your gifts one of the central purposes of your life will become exponentially more difficult and challenging, especially as you ascend the planes of mastery. The higher a level of mastery you achieve, the more discipline, sacrifice and austerity will be required to reach the "next level" of mastery. A man who has never lifted weights before can add triple digits to some of his lifts within the span of a year of casual training. A world-class powerlifter may add just *one* pound to his previous record in that same year, despite hundreds of times the level of effort, skill, and intensity.

Will you have the *discipline* to remain on the path of mastering your gifts when grinding out tiny increments of mastery becomes so difficult that almost all your competitors hit a wall at that same point of resistance? Developing and exercising your gifts is not about having "fun" or being "entertained". Following your purpose in life by developing your great gifts is anything but passive recreation: in fact, doing so will inevitably lead to intense pain and suffering: yes, *following your purpose in life will lead to pain and suffering.*

IV. Purpose

The Nobility of Pain

One of the great lies of the Dark-Age of Decadence is that pain is to be avoided at all costs and that suffering is meaningless and must be therefore extinguished at the first signs. This is the emergent "Religion of Comfortableness" that Nietzsche observed in his day, which has since grown to dominate the entire *weltanschauung* of contemporary Western culture in this Neo-Dark Age.

Yet it is pain and suffering itself that elevates life to the spiritual heights of nobility! Would climbing a mountain be an impressive feat if there were no pain, suffering, agony, danger, and potential for death involved in the endeavour? No. Just because you are naturally talented in a particular set of skills, just because you have a gift, does not mean that the development of it, the mastery of it, is going to be "easy" – *and do not lament this fact either, but embrace it!*

This is why the Neo-Peasant has no significant accomplishments to boast of; he quits as soon as obstacles are inevitably encountered and crawls back into his petty cocoon of entertainment, comfort and distraction in order to avoid experiencing pain. Yet, one throbbing existential ache always remains: *the suffering of he who does not have a definitive sense of purpose in his life.*

The man who endeavours to continue developing his gift despite all the obstacles and challenges that he will inevitably meet, though his body may ache, and though he may be adorned by the scars of battle, *he is at least liberated of the greatest suffering of all: the purposeless life.*

Your Gift is Your Destiny

Your gift may inspire the selection of a related Arch-Mission which serves as the practical, objective outlet for the pursuit and development of your natural talents. However, the sense of *meaning* provided by your Purpose inspired Missions is not ultimately derived from their actual achievement or accomplishment, specifically: *it is resultant of the fact that you are pursuing your destiny.*

The calling of your gift emanates from within the heart of your personal Omega-Point of Purpose: it is your North Star – it guides you in the dead of night, but is never actually arrived at. Surrender the lie that life is ever "complete". This is the beauty of your *gift:* it can never be depleted; it will *always* provide meaning in your life, so long as you are willing to sacrifice the false-idols of the "Religion of Comfortableness" that have come to dominate the Dark-Age of Decadence.

Instead, embrace the nobility of pursuing your personal evolution and commit to developing your gifts: *this is your Purpose as a Neo-Renaissance Man.*

IV. Purpose

ii. Personal Mythology

Every culture invariably develops a unique MYTHOLOGY: stories and parables that express the culture's guiding moral principles, or which encapsulate wisdom and lessons that were deemed sacred enough to be preserved for the benefit of future generations. Mythological stories are not meant to be *literal* interpretations of the past; it is the *lessons* that matter, as they serve to guide men toward nobility and deter them from commonly observed pitfalls and traps.

Mythologies are cultural guides to morality. While the details of the stories themselves are not literally true, mythological beliefs, *if internalized as if they are true*, serve as useful moral and behavioural compasses. Mythologies allow you to refer to the lessons of your ancestors in order to properly orient yourself when faced with difficult moral decisions or seemingly insurmountable obstacles.

"Why?"

Mythologies provide a culture with a sense of existential *meaning*, for they provide answers to the fundamental question of life: "*Why?*"

Why bother to "become a Neo-Renaissance Man" at all? *Why not* just enjoy the frivolous comforts and distractions of the Dark-Age of Decadence? *Why* bother with confronting obstacles, hardship or adversity at all? *Why not* avoid all suffering? *Why not* accept mediocrity and merge into the formlessness of Mass Man? *Why not surrender to becoming a Neo-Peasant and just settle for an easy life of comfort, convenience and pleasure?*

For the man whose lip quivers with these ignoble cries of antipathy, there is no rational answer, no objective response: you cannot logically convince this man that he must assume an attitude of Responsibility; or that he must endeavour to forge a Vision for his life; or stress that he must become a Mission oriented man-of-action.

No, for this man, for this nihilist, the only possible rebuttal is to evoke within him his dormant *mythological spirit*. Only Mythology can sufficiently express *why* a man should embrace the difficult but noble life of a Neo-Renaissance Man.

This is why the Neo-Renaissance Man is a serial collector of mythological stories that particularly resonate with him and which invoke this aforementioned 'mythological spirit'. These stories collectively form what could be described as a PERSONAL MYTHLOGY. The object is to then orient your behavior and actions *as if* these mythologies were true, treating the metaphysical or moral implications of the stories with a religious deference.

The Myth of Sisyphus

The creation of a Personal Mythology – a private pantheon of highly esteemed mythological parables, stories and beliefs – is your own responsibility. The journey is as important as the destination. However, by way of example, there are two stories in particular that provide the Neo-Renaissance Man with a sense of *mythological context* – a moral and philosophical justification – for his chosen life path.

IV. Purpose

The first guiding myth of the Neo-Renaissance Man is courtesy of the ancient Greeks, who are famous for their innate sense of mythological vision. *The Myth of Sisyphus* is one such story that, in particular, is uniquely meaningful to the Neo-Renaissance Man.

In the myth, Sisyphus is a king who is punished by the gods for certain indiscretions: he is condemned to roll a boulder up a mountain only to hopeless witness it roll back down again when he finally reaches the top – and he is cursed to repeat this cycle *eternally*. In the modern lexicon, the word "Sisyphean" has therefore become an adjective synonymous with utter futility. A "Sisyphean fate" is one that is repetitive, laborious and difficult, yet which is also entirely fruitless, producing nothing of value.

However, in the 1950's there was a French philosopher, Albert Camus, who published a book called *The Myth of Sisyphus* in which he challenged the traditional interpretation of the myth and substituted his own unique perspective. For Camus, the fate of Sisyphus was certainly tragic, *but he also detected an implicit sense of hope in the story*.

"The struggle itself toward the heights," wrote Camus, "is enough to fill a man's heart." Camus argued that since every single day Sisyphus had a singular, definitive objective to dedicate himself to – *because he had a purpose* – that what was intended to be hell inadvertently became his "silent joy."

Camus's interpretation of the myth extracts elemental purpose from what is seemingly the ultimate adversity. "His fate belongs to him," explained Camus, "His rock is his thing." In this way, the explicit despair of the original myth is transformed into tragic yet defiant hope. "One must imagine Sisyphus happy," concluded Camus in the final lines of his book.

Camus's contrarian reinterpretation of the Myth of Sisyphus is an excellent example of how traditional mythologies may be creatively adapted in ways that personally resonate with you. For the Neo-Renaissance Man, Camus's interpretation of the Sisyphus myth mirrors his own eternal, never satisfied striving for self-mastery and personal evolution.

Nobility is *Sisyphean*

Self-command and continuous personal development are ongoing processes, not end-states: they are your Sisyphean task, your "rock", that you perpetually roll up the mountain everyday, knowing full-well that you will have to repeat the whole process again tomorrow, and the next day, and so on until death itself. In other words: *the path of the Neo-Renaissance Man is inherently Sisyphean in nature*, according to Camus's philosophical interpretation of the myth.

The Neo-Peasant however, the instant he realizes that commitment to the Four Pillars of The Neo-Renaissance Man is permanent, the moment he realizes that *the life of inner-nobility is inherently, incontrovertibly Sisyphean in nature*, he abandons responsibility for his own personal evolution and instead allows himself to be spiritually sublimated into the "Religion of Comfortableness" that is The Church of this Dark-Age of Decadence.

Yes: the life of great men, of Ascetic-Noblemen, is inherently Sisyphean. Yet, for the Neo-Renaissance Man, is that not a "silent joy", as Camus described it? *Your personal evolution will never end!* You just keep pushing your rock up that mountain, every day: you become better today than you were yesterday, and better tomorrow than you are today. This is your Purpose. You, like Sisyphus, "one must imagine happy", and it is through the creative interpretation and internalization of mythology that allows one to imagine thus.

Eternal Recurrence

It is not only ancient myths that resonate with the life of the Neo-Renaissance Man, however. The myth of Sisyphus is ancient. Others are modern. Friedrich Nietzsche, the nineteenth-century philosopher who was one of the first to recognize the fateful dawning of the Dark-Age of Decadence, was the author of several philosophical parables that could be described as modern mythological stories.

Nietzsche's magnum opus, *Thus Spoke Zarathustra*, is perhaps the penultimate modern example of the medium of mythology being leveraged in order to convey fundamental lessons about the meaning of life. *Zarathustra* is an entire book written in the mythological style, and it is clear that Nietzsche was keenly aware of the resonant power of mythology to inspire men. A mythological story does not have to be a long one, like *Zarathustra*, however. It may also come in the form of a short but potent parable.

One of the most haunting and spiritually jarring of these short mythological parables is Nietzsche's famous parable of Eternal Recurrence. Found buried in his criminally overlooked book *The Gay Science*, a collection of maxims, principles, and other such mythological parables, Nietzsche's Eternal Recurrence allegory is an example of how mythology can radically influence how one interprets the mystery and meaning of life. Eternal Recurrence:

> *"The greatest weight – What, if some day or night a demon were to steal after you into your loneliest loneliness and say to you:*
> *This life as you now live it and have lived it, you will have to live once more and innumerable times more; and there will be nothing new in it, but every pain and every joy and every thought and sigh and everything unutterably small or great in your life will have to return to you, all in the same succession and sequence - even this spider and this moonlight between the trees, and even this moment and I myself. The eternal hourglass of existence is turned upside down again and again, and you with it, speck of dust!"*
> *Would you not throw yourself down and gnash your teeth and curse the demon who spoke thus?... Or how well disposed would you have to become to yourself and to life to crave nothing more fervently than this ultimate eternal confirmation and seal?"*

For the Neo-Renaissance Man, is this not a towering literary passage? How life affirming – or existentially terrifying, depending on your perspective – a single idea can be, and how effective the medium of mythology can be in delivering such vivid imagery. Imagine that "some day or night" that you *did* have a fateful encounter with Nietzsche's mythological demon who confronted you with this prospect of Eternal Recurrence – *and what if the implications were a metaphysical reality?*

Regret

Why do you choose to make the sacrifices you do to become a Neo-Renaissance Man? Why do you choose the pain and suffering of pursuing self-mastery and personal evolution over the comfort and luxury of the inertial life of a Neo-Peasant? Why do you bother becoming a Neo-

Renaissance Man at all? Why? Because, as Nietzsche's myth of Eternal Recurrence so forcibly provokes us into considering, REGRET is the most gnawing, torturous, permanent curse that a man can cast upon himself.

Regret that we wasted our lives frittering away our time in order to avoid our most basic responsibilities; *regret* that we did not endeavor to create a vivid vision for who we are, who we want to become, and what our legacy will be; *regret* that we pursued no great missions or crusades; *regret* that we did not live lives of genuine meaning and purpose – regret, in other words, *that we chose to waste our potential for nobility and settled for being average, common, mediocre men.*

Nietzsche vividly reminds us of the danger of regret, the danger of a life "unlived", of any moment unlived – for, as he so terrifyingly proposes in his myth of Eternal Recurrence, *what if* you were fated to relive every single one of your decisions again, exactly as they occurred, an infinite number of times? *What if* those were the stakes? *What if Eternal Recurrence was a metaphysical reality and every decision you made had to be filtered through that criterion?* Would you be able to live with the decisions that you have made *if you had to relive them an infinite number of times?*

Life Affirming Mythology

For the Neo-Renaissance Man, who believes that his legacy echoes into eternity, and who lives his life as such, Nietzsche's parable is full of resounding hope, affirmation and joy. For the Neo-Peasant, who at the end of his life realizes that he was duped by this "Great Age", that he wasted his inertial life with frivolous entertainment and empty distractions, Nietzsche's myth of Eternal Recurrence may as well be a description of hell.

This is the power of Mythology: it has the ability to overlay meaningful meta-narratives onto the context of your life that radiate the energy of purpose *to the degree that you successfully internalize the underlying lessons of the myths – to the extent, in other words, that you believe them.* Literal belief in these mythological stories is obviously not required, yet you must model your behaviour *as if* the stories were true and literally applicable to your life.

To live *as if* the mythologies that influence your life – the stories, lessons, principles, and beliefs that you recognize uncommon wisdom in – are true, *this is how the Neo-Renaissance Man saturates his life with the spiritual substance of purpose.* If you believe that you live in a "meaningless", "purposeless" universe, then *you* do. If, through the power of mythology, you come to believe that the universe is overflowing with purpose, then for you, *it does.*

iii. Meta-Purpose

The Forth Pillar of the Neo-Renaissance Man is that of Purpose. The Principle of Purpose is a trinity composed of three categorical types of Purpose: *Your Gift* and *Personal Mythology* have been already studied, so that leaves the final member of the triad, META-PURPOSE, which shall be the subject of this chapter.

Elemental Purpose

Your Meta-Purpose is your deepest purpose as a man. It can never be taken away from you, and its fulfillment can never be denied to you by anyone but yourself. It is the *prime substance* of all other forms of purpose in your life. It is the 'granular atom', so to speak, of Purpose: it can arrange itself in an infinite number of ways, producing a multitude of different structures and forms of "purpose", *yet at root it always remains the same fundamental material.*

Within the structure of the Four Pillars of the Neo-Renaissance Man, there is a great degree of variability in regards to the specific context or application of each principle. The unique context of the lives of individual men will obviously vary to a considerable degree.

However, all the Neo-Renaissance Men of our age *do* share one basic Meta-Purpose that links them together; one singular, common Purpose that collectively defines their shared *raisen d'etre;* it is the same secret yet self-evident Purpose that all living beings share – in fact, it is actually the Purpose of the very cosmos itself:

Evolution

It is EVOLUTION that is the Omega-Point of all life, the Meta-Purpose of all existence. To grow, to change, to improve, to master: all living creatures are guided by this Great Principle, by this *reason to live,* to strive, to fight, to struggle, to thrive!

Humans are the only beings that we know of that are *aware* of this process of evolution, however, and this places our species in the unique position of being able to *consciously and intentionally direct the process.* We are not only capable of becoming self-aware of our ultimate Meta-Purpose, but we actually are able to *influence* the process! This should be an astonishing, miraculous revelation to anyone who perceives the awesome implications of this fact.

The Neo-Renaissance Man is fundamentally the Man of Evolution: he is driven by the ultimate aim of SELF-MASTERY, which is really just another word for "conscious evolution". In all circumstances he lives his life with this reason, this purpose as a guiding force. The Neo-Renaissance Man has trained himself to be ever aware of this sacred Meta-Purpose, and all his actions, behaviours, beliefs and attitudes ultimately spawn from this eternal teleological wellspring.

Retrogression and the Neo-Peasant

However, if it is true that humans are the only beings that are aware of this singular Meta-Purpose of all life, and are therefore the only beings that can assert conscious influence upon the process of their own evolution, *it is also inversely the case that humans are the only beings who can actively choose to refuse to evolve.*

IV. Purpose

It is a great paradox: men, who are given this greatest of gifts – consciousness of their own ability to evolve – as well as the freewill to utilize that gift in whatever form they choose, are also the same beings who all too often choose the *opposite* of evolution: RETROGRESSION, the return to less complex or primitive states of existence.

The Neo-Peasant, the archetypal personification of this Dark-Age of Decadence, is in the final analysis the Man of Inertia: he chooses to ignore his own personal evolution and instead shipwrecks his life onto the desert shores of inertial stagnation. He is forever "stuck" because he refuses to accept that adversity, pain, and suffering are the gold-standard of all organic growth and evolution, and payment is *always* due up-front and in full.

The Neo-Peasant chooses instead to live the opposite of a life of perpetual striving toward self-mastery and personal evolution by surrounding himself with the Faustian comforts, luxuries, and distractions enticingly offered by the Dark-Age of Decadence. Then he ironically complains that his life feels "empty"; that there is "no meaning to life"; that the universe has "no purpose".

In order to at least temporarily repress the horrors of these dark existential thoughts, the Neo-Peasant plunges further into the abyss of self-distraction: he avoids his responsibilities, ignores his lack of ambition, and by submerging himself in a heroin stupor of decadent self-indulgence he in essence attempts to suspend time itself, and in doing so implicitly denies the reality of his own mortality.

The Neo-Peasant escapes further and further into the dim corridors of his private *Versailles*, his furtive Palace of Distraction, attempting in every way to insulate himself from the secret fact that he dares not admit to himself:

that his sacred Meta-Purpose as a man is to EVOLVE: to become better today than he was yesterday, and better tomorrow than he is today; to become a disciple of self-mastery; to relentlessly pursue the masculine Meta-Purpose of Evolution.

The Retrogression of the West

Indeed, it is now all too painfully obvious that the entire edifice of Western Civilization has chosen wilfully the path of retrogression. This is why we elect to call this present epoch in the history of Western Civilization the *Dark-Age of Decadence*.

The carnival sideshow that Western Civilization has been rapidly degenerating into is no substitute for living a life dedicated to the Forth Pillar of the Neo-Renaissance Man: Purpose. The innumerable 'existential avoidance mechanisms' offered by the Dark-Age of Decadence will never succeed in making men feel that their lives are deeply fulfilled, no matter how technologically "advanced" they become: *hollow distractions and trivial pursuits have never, and never will, fill the gaping crater left in a man's soul when his Meta-Purpose in life is perpetually neglected.* There is no substitute for genuine purpose. There is no avoiding the necessity of pursuing your own personal evolution.

Full-immersion "virtual reality" technology is presently developing at an exponential pace: escapism and avoidance of reality shall be so effectively enabled by this technology that legions of men will be forever lost to these digital illusions. "Virtual reality" presents itself as seemingly the ultimate solution to the Neo-Peasant's gnawing existential malaise, *but it will only make it worse by further amplifying his retrogressive disconnection from his Meta-Purpose.*

Evolve!

To become a Neo-Renaissance Man is quintessentially to recognize that your Meta-Purpose as a man is to strive toward self-mastery and consciously guide and influence your personal evolution – *everything else of value and utility in a man's life flows from that recognition.*

When a man finally realizes what his ultimate Meta-Purpose is it *justifies* the adversity he inevitably encounters, the obstacles he shall confront, and the pain and suffering that he will surely endure. Escape the infernal dogma of the "Religion of Comfortableness" and finally be liberated from the chains of the Dark-Age of Decadence that have shackled you from the pursuit of his own personal evolution.

Conclusion

PURPOSE, for the Neo-Renaissance Man, in all its forms, is the great guiding Omega-Point of his life: he is drawn to it, compelled by it, and attracted toward it. To *know* Purpose, however, you must not be distracted; you must watch and listen in stillness and silence: you must practice the sacred discipline of AUSTERITY.

Austerity

If you still have no distinct feeling or sense of the Forth Pillar of the Neo-Renaissance Man, Purpose, even after reading and reflecting upon the preceding chapters, *then you must take radical action and mercilessly eliminate the distractions that continue to cloud your spiritual vision from recognizing what should be a luminescent North Star pulsing in the starry night sky of your soul.*

Austerity is the elimination of the non-essential, the superfluous, the decadent; it is the sacrifice of comfort and entertainment so that you may gain vision and clarity. Whatever *distractions* you are relying upon to avoid the discovery and pursuit of Purpose are those that must be ruthlessly eliminated.

If you cannot clearly *feel* exactly what your purpose in life is, then you must enter into a mode of austere living: eliminate the distractions in your life, *all of them*, and then remain still, just *"be"* – listening, watching, feeling, until your Omega-Point reveals itself to you, until your spiritual vision adjusts and brings into clear focus an elemental sense of *purpose*.

Purpose is a Responsibility

The Neo-Renaissance Man lives in a deeply purposeful, meaningful universe. The Neo-Peasant does not. "The meaning of life" is what we make it: this is the plainly obvious answer to that most ancient, perennial question.

In this Dark-Age of Decadence however, the average man expects "purpose" to be delivered to him with the same ease and convenience as ordering a pizza. It does not work that way: *Purpose is a responsibility, not a right; it is a duty, not a commodity.* Most men fail to grasp this fundamental truth, and their derelict lives are organic monuments to this fact.

It is the rare man who recognizes that it is his own personal responsibility to seek out his deepest Purpose, to discover it, and then to dedicate his life toward following its eternal guiding light. Become that rare man. *Become the Neo-Renaissance Man.*

Afterward

> *"Principle — An inescapable hypothesis to which humanity must have recourse again and again is more powerful in the long run than the most firmly believed faith in an untruth... In the long run: that means in this context a hundred thousand years."*
>
> — Friedrich Nietzsche

THE Four Pillars of the Neo-Renaissance Man — *Responsibility, Vision, Mission,* and *Purpose* — represent the distillation of the eternal principles of masculine self-mastery into their most elemental form. They are as applicable in this Dark-Age of Decadence as they were for our distant ancestors, and they will be just as germane to the future Disciples of Self-Mastery, in whatever cultural incarnations they may appear in millennia to come.

The Ancient Tradition of Nobility

True "Noble Men" have gone by different names throughout history: during the Renaissance, they were *Renaissance Men;* during this present era, the Dark-Age of Decadence, we refer to them as the *Neo-Renaissance Men*; and during other ages and epochs, these Few have gone by other designations – *but they have always been rightfully recognized for their exceptionality, for being fundamentally different than the average, common man.* They are not "noble" because of inherited class distinctions or titles or privilege, but because of their rarely witnessed *nobility* of attitude, behaviour and conduct.

The unifying relationship between this rare class of men across time and space is their adherence to certain *eternal principles*. These principles are not secret; they are open and accessible to all men. Yet, because so few men seek *truth* when it comes to discovering the process by which they may become self-sovereign masters of their lives, these eternal principles seem to escape them: the average man just want the "quick fix", the solution that requires no effort, work or sacrifice. Shortcuts are actually detours, and if you take enough of them you will become hopelessly lost – stay on *The Path* and you will never lose your way.

The eternal principles of self-mastery, described through the vehicle of this book, *Four Pillars of the Neo-Renaissance Man*, represent the only true path toward becoming a masculine, grounded, poised man – to becoming a Neo-Renaissance Man. The reason so few seem to be aware of the power of knowing – no, of *living* – these principles is because *The Four Pillars* are not a "magic pill": they represent a lifestyle, a discipline, *a way of life* that few men are willing to adopt as a permanent disposition.

The traditional Ascetic-Noblemen of history, and the Neo-Renaissance Man of this Dark-Age of Decadence, remain exceptional because they are so rare. Perhaps this is why when you meet someone who is *clearly* a "Neo-Renaissance Man" they are instantly monumentalized in our memory.

If you were to describe to any of these men of genuine inner-nobility the Four Pillars of the Neo-Renaissance Man – even if they have not read this book – their reply would surely be, *"Well, of course . . ."* The Four Pillars are PRINCIPLES, in the Nietzschean sense: *as true today as they were ten thousand years ago, and as true as they will be in future epochs of history.*

Tough Love

Of course, the inverse is also true, then: there shall always be masses of men, the vast majority in fact, who refuse to live lives of vital action or focused contemplation; men who refuse to *evolve,* to change, to improve; men for whom "self-mastery" is antithetical to their arch-desire for safety, comfort and the avoidance of pain. These are the Men of Retrogression. This book is not written for these men, and if they were to read it, they would find it insulting, condescending, even blasphemous. It was not written with any of these intentions, but it was also not censored in order to protect their feelings, shield their honour, or compromise the truth.

The reason for the cold, often harsh, and unforgiving character of this book is that some men require tough love: men who are living *like* Neo-Peasants, *like* the average masses, mesmerized by distractions, pampered into spiritual oblivion by comfort and luxury. These men for whom this book was written are living *as if* they were archetypical Neo-Peasants, *but this is not their true self!*

The archetype of the Neo-Renaissance Men is dormant within them, just waiting to be liberated, to be unleashed – *if only they would awaken from their slumber long enough to take heed of how mediocre and sorry their lives have become!* These men must be *shocked* out of complacency, even if that means wounding their pride or offending the sensibilities of the masses.

The lesson of this book is not that one small, exclusive class of men is inherently "better" than the masses: it is that most men *choose* not to join this elite aristocracy of self-sovereign noblemen by their own volition! They can choose to transcend their own mediocrity *at any time*; they can choose to become great men, to revolutionize their lives, *at any time*.

The power to utterly transform your life in the instant of a moment, and then to remain on that path of personal evolution as a permanent way of life, is real. *Any man can become a Neo-Renaissance Man at any time.* This is his sovereign blood-right as a *man* . . . and it is his own damned responsibility if he chooses to deny it.

Self-Mastery in the Age of Western Collapse

Definitively resolve to become a Neo-Renaissance Man: ignore the distractions and temptations of the Dark-Age of Decadence and be ever vigilant of the corrupting influence of its governing "Religion of Comfortableness". Beware of the material abundance and luxurious indulgences of our age, which *appear* to signal the arrival of a "Golden Age", yet which are actually the catabolic forces that shall transmute technological progress and material abundance into the seeds of cultural decadence, decline, and collapse.

This is a Dark Age: indeed, so dark that few men seem capable of recognizing the death spiral that the organism of The West has fatally locked into. The prevailing culture of the Dark-Age of Decadence is so enamoured with its own comforts, luxuries, and the material abundance of *everything* that it appears to be incapable of recognizing the sinister shadow that has been cast upon us all, *the shadow of a horrific fate for Western Civilization that we are rapidly accelerating toward.*

All a man can do in such fateful historical context is to stoically serve as a witness to the decline and collapse of his once noble culture and civilization, and to take personal responsibility for keeping its Promethean spirit alive in his own life, at least. Do not become a Man of Fate, the Neo-Peasant, the road-kill of history, passively shaped and moulded by the influences of his toxic cultural environment. That is all that a man can do in these grim circumstances.

The Neo-Peasant

A traditional "peasant" is he who is externally denied nobility and who often struggles to provide the basic necessities of survival; there is no shame in this fate, as it is not this sort of peasant's choice to endure such oppression and hardship.

The "peasant" of our contemporary age, however, denies *himself* nobility and struggles not with material deprivation but rather with material abundance, which he is wholly incapable of handling in a responsible, noble fashion. The Neo-Peasant represents a great inversion of historical roles, as now it is the common, average man who lives like a king, *but without nobility of character!*

The Neo-Peasant is a broken man, enslaved by his own unwillingness to stage a great insurrection within himself in order to reclaim his sovereign right of *self-command*. He drags his feet through life: no sense of

Purpose; no definitive Mission; totally void of Vision; and entirely dismissive of even his most basic Responsibilities: this man does not even know what he is going to do with himself this afternoon, let alone a decade from now.

A peasant floats through history like a leaf in the wind, asserting little influence upon its own destiny, entirely the subject of the winds of fate, and periodically crushed by the cyclical forces of history. So too for the average man of our age, the Neo-Peasant: he is the product of his historical era – the Dark-Age of Decadence, the Empire of Distraction, the Epoch of Comfort, Luxury and Avarice – in which all may live as kings, *but feel like miserable, directionless, powerless peasants.*

The Neo-Renaissance Man

Stop behaving like most men. Do not let your life become or remain an archetypical incarnation of the Neo-Peasant here described. *Be your own man.* Become master of your *self.* Take control of the process of evolution, which is your sacred and divine Meta-Purpose as a man. Liberate your spirit from the poverty of the Dark-Age of Decadence and reclaim your sovereign right of nobility.

Join the tradition of Ascetic-Nobility: endeavour to forge a *new* Age of Nobility in which wealth is defined not by luxurious comfort and the ubiquity of mass-distraction, *but by the measure of discipline, ambition and passion that a man has bursting from his heart.*

There shall be a new age following the inevitable collapse of the present one: it shall be an age of rebirth, of renewal; an age in which the few men of nobility remaining rise from the ashes of a dead civilization in order to build a new one, a better one. This shall be the NEO-RENAISSANCE.

Afterward

The Eternal Principles of Self-Mastery

The Neo-Renaissance Age shall be built upon the foundational Four Pillars, the eternal principles of self-mastery and personal evolution:

I. RESPONSABILITY
II. VISION
III. MISSION
IV. PURPOSE

Without the support of the Pillar of Responsibility, no further ambition is possible; the smallest duty sufficiently ignored denies the greatest accomplishments. You must, first, *take responsibility* for your life, in every context, and make this a permanent disposition of your character.

Then, the Pillar of Vision becomes accessible. Without *Vision,* a man does not know who he is *now,* let alone who he wants to *become*, or what *legacy* he intends to create. Vision is the fuel of motivation, passion and white-hot burning desire. Vision is where dreams are forged.

The Pillar of Mission converts creative vision into concrete reality. *Mission* is where you wage war to accomplish your dreams. This is the stuff of crusade, conquest and victory. Every man must be a warrior. Become a Man of Action.

Then there is the final Pillar of Purpose: without a sense of *meaning* in life, there is no point in erecting the first three pillars. Without a great Omega-Point to guide you, life becomes cold and hostile, and nihilistic fatalism creeps into your psyche. *Purpose* is the great elevator of all the other Pillars, unifying them collectively into a mutually supporting structure. Without Purpose, the other three

Pillars would not be "pillars" at all . . . but rather petty heaps of meaningless, lifeless rocks.

The *Four Pillars of the Neo-Renaissance Man:* the foundational structure for any man who endeavours toward self-mastery in his life. These are *original* principles, not in the sense that this book has invented them, but in the sense that they are primeval. Indeed, *these principles invented this book*, not the other way around.

If you wish to stop living a petty, mediocre, unfulfilling life – if you recognize only *yourself* when the archetype of the Neo-Peasant is described – *then this is The Way, this is The Path* toward liberating yourself from the tyranny of your own self-imposed inertial life of decadence and distraction. Break free from the inertia of the Dark-Age of Decadence and definitively endeavour to become . . .

A NEO-RENAISSANCE MAN.

Acknowledgements

I consider myself to be immeasurably fortunate to have been blessed with my mother and father. Fortune can be won, success can be achieved, but to have loving, supportive parents is a gift that can only be humbly received. It has been only later in life that I have come to understand how challenging it must be to raise a child in a world of corrupting influences and poisonous ideas. I thank them for their courage and dedication as parents.

To my brother Marc, I appreciate the sharpened sense of logic and rationality that I have been able to hone through our many conversations and debates over the years.

My brother Timothy is a quintessential *Neo-Renaissance Man*. If Western Civilization is to survive, it will be men like Timothy that save it. I have your *six*, brother, and always will.

Finally, I thank my girlfriend Alyssa, who encouraged me to complete this project in a creative way that few women would ever have thought of, yet alone actually endeavoured to accomplish.

About the Author

Eric Deslauriers is an active-duty military officer. The manuscript for this book was written while recovering from a training-related injury and subsequent surgery. Eric resides in New Brunswick, Canada as of 2019.

Contact: neo-renaissanceman@protonmail.com

Made in the USA
Columbia, SC
16 November 2020